THE FOLLOWING BOOK IS DEDICATED

TO MY MOTHER

AND TO THE MEMORY OF MY FATHER.

Twayne's United States Authors Series

Sylvia E. Bowman, *Editor*

INDIANA UNIVERSITY

Catharine Maria Sedgwick

CATHARINE MARIA SEDGWICK

By EDWARD HALSEY FOSTER

The Stevens Institute of Technology

 233

Twayne Publishers, Inc.   ::   New York

Library of Congress Cataloging in Publication Data

Foster, Edward Halsey.
    Catharine Maria Sedgwick.

    (Twayne's United States authors series, TUSAS 233)
    Bibliography: p.
    1. Sedgwick, Catharine Maria, 1789–1867.
PS2798.Z5F6 1974   813'.2   73–14674
ISBN 0–8057–0658–5

Preface

To many mid-nineteenth-century critics who sought a thriving American literature, the novels of Catharine Maria Sedgwick seemed to be as significant as works by her distinguished contemporaries, James Fenimore Cooper, William Cullen Bryant, and Washington Irving. It is unlikely today that her didactic tales and her volumes of moral instruction for children will receive any serious consideration in studies of early American literature, but our more recent literary histories of the period should have reconsidered those early Sedgwick novels—notably *Redwood* (1824) and *Hope Leslie* (1827)—that were so highly praised both in this country and in England. However, surprisingly few modern critics appear to have heard of either novel, and even fewer seem to have read them.

In this examination of Miss Sedgwick's works, I find that they deserve more attention from students of American literature than they usually receive. For one thing, Miss Sedgwick was a far more successful stylist than Cooper, the most famous of early American novelists. She also had a greater ability in creating believable women in her fiction than any of her contemporary American authors—a fact which should be of special interest in view of today's studies of women in literature. Indeed, although she could create women as vapid and uninteresting as some of Cooper's females—as, for example, the character of Gertrude Clarence in Miss Sedgwick's *Clarence* (1830)—her heroines in *Redwood* and in *Hope Leslie* are fully realized, flesh-and-blood women in an age when most women in fiction seldom seemed quite mortal. Furthermore, although she provided each of her heroines with a suitable husband, she wrote *Married or Single?* to show that marriage was not essential for the happiness of every woman—an opinion which was by no means universally accepted when the novel was published in 1857.

In this study, I also demonstrate Miss Sedgwick's importance as a novelist of manners. *Redwood* is in part a study of American manners, and both *Clarence* and *Married or Single?* involve criticism of the manners of aristocrats in New York. Furthermore, I show that much of Miss Sedgwick's fiction—not all of it distinguished as literature—provides important examinations of American civilization from the viewpoint of one who sincerely believed in the Jeffersonian ideal: an agricultural Republic controlled by an aristocracy of talent and virtue. Likewise, she welcomed Jacksonian emphasis on the common man; and *The Linwoods*—published in 1835 while Andrew Jackson was still in office—concludes with the marriage of the son of a poor farmer to the daughter of a New York aristocrat. Miss Sedgwick's Jeffersonian sentiments are at the center of *Clarence*, which contrasts the aristocracy of wealth with the aristocracy of talent and virtue.

In addition, I examine Miss Sedgwick's importance as a regionalist—her abilities in detailing New England history and landscape as well as manners and customs. Throughout many of her novels and didactic tales, Miss Sedgwick made considerable use of her New England background. I demonstrate, however, that Miss Sedgwick was much more than a regionalist concerned only with New England; *Redwood*, for example, introduces Southerners as well as Yankees among the central characters; and *Clarence* is about New York. Although Miss Sedgwick concentrated on New England, she was a writer with national as well as regional interests.

The biographical information which I include serves various purposes: first, it demonstrates Miss Sedgwick's heavy dependence on her own experience for the materials of her fiction; second, it documents her considerable reputation among her contemporaries. Furthermore, it suggests the importance of her brothers as critics of her writing and as her literary agents who found publishers

for her writings and handled the financial aspects of publishing. Few records survive to tell us exactly how much
they helped her; but, if her statements are to be believed,
her debt to them was enormous. I also include information
on the American Lake District, as the mid-nineteenth-century
community of writers in Western Massachusetts was called.
Among the most significant writers in this community were
Oliver Wendell Holmes, Henry Wadsworth Longfellow,
Nathaniel Hawthorne, and Herman Melville; and Miss
Sedgwick was one of the better-known members of this
group.

Hope Leslie and *Redwood* have been republished recently by the Garrett Press, and a handful of studies of
Miss Sedgwick's works have appeared during the last
dozen or so years, but even her most important novels
remain generally unknown to most students of literature.
Her historical importance, as this study demonstrates,
is irrefutable; and at least two of her works, the republished
Redwood and *Hope Leslie,* demand serious attention as
literature. In brief, no American author of her time was
more successful in the creation of women in fiction; few
were her equals as novelists of manners; and, among her
contemporaries, none sketched as credible a picture of
Yankee New England.

EDWARD HALSEY FOSTER

Newport and New York City

Acknowledgments

This study was suggested to me many years ago by William Cullen Bryant, III, who, while working on a study of his poet-ancestor, had searched for information about Miss Sedgwick, one of Bryant's closest associates. In preparing this study, I found especially valuable the encouragement of Professor Joseph V. Ridgely of Columbia University and Professor Lewis Leary of the University of North Carolina; Professor Leary's criticism of Chapter 6 was much needed and appreciated. I am deeply indebted to Professor Carl Hovde of Columbia College who devoted considerable time to reading early drafts of this book and to suggesting improvements. Professor R. Jackson Wilson of Smith College also read the manuscript and offered helpful suggestions. Any errors of judgment or fact in this book are, of course, my own responsibility.

I would like to express appreciation for the expert typing of Mrs. Hilda McArthur and Mrs. Thurza Small. I am indebted to my mother for driving me to the original locations of many scenes described in the Sedgwick novels. Above all, I owe particular thanks to Elaine, who has endured seemingly endless discussions and drafts of this book. And then, too, our daughter and son have spent many quiet hours while this study was written.

Contents

Chronology

1785   Sedgwick family settled in Stockbridge, Massachusetts.

1789   Catharine Maria Sedgwick born December 28, the ninth of ten children, including Theodore (b. 1780), Henry Dwight (b. 1785), Robert (b. 1787), and Charles (b. 1791); daughter of Theodore Sedgwick, Speaker of the United States House of Representatives during the administration of George Washington.

1813   Death of her father.

1820   Met William Cullen Bryant, the beginning of a close friendship that continued throughout her life.

1821   Joined the Unitarian Church.

1822   Published *A New-England Tale,* originally intended as a religious tract for Unitarians.

1824   Published *Redwood,* her first major work.

1825   *Redwood* reviewed by Bryant for *The North American Review.*

1827   Published *Hope Leslie,* her best-known novel.

1828-   Deaths of Elizabeth Freeman and Henry Dwight
1835   Sedgwick. Moved to Lenox, Massachusetts, to live with her brother Charles, whose wife had opened a school for girls.

1830   Published *Clarence.*

1832   Beginning of friendship with Fanny Kemble, Shakespearean actress.

1835   Published *The Linwoods*.

1835- Published *Home, The Poor Rich Man and The Rich
1837   Poor Man,* and *Live and Let Live,* a trilogy of didactic tales and her most popular books.

1835- The years during which the American Lake District
1860   was especially popular with American writers.

1839- Traveled in Europe.
1840

1841   Published *Letters from Abroad to Kindred at Home*.

1848   Published *The Boy of Mount Rhigi*.

1855   Death of brother Charles.

1857   Published *Married or Single?*, her last novel.

1858   Published *Memoir of Joseph Curtis,* her last book.

1865   Visited Stockbridge for the last time; remainder of her life spent principally in the home of a niece outside Boston.

1867   Died July 31; buried in Stockbridge cemetery with her brothers and parents.

1871   *Life and Letters* published.

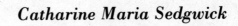

Catharine Maria Sedgwick

CHAPTER *1*

The Berkshire Brahmins

There is . . . in New England, an aristocracy, if you choose to call it so. . . . It has grown to be a *caste*,—not in any odious sense, —but, by the repetition of the same influences, generation after generation, it has acquired a distinct organization and physiognomy, which not to recognize is mere stupidity, and not to be willing to describe would show a distrust of the good-nature and intelligence of our readers, who like to have us see all we can and tell all we see.

— Oliver Wendell Holmes[1]

I *The American Lake District*

NEAR the banks of the Housatonic River in the southern reaches of the Berkshire hills in Western Massachusetts are the villages of Stockbridge and Lenox. The region is a pastoral setting of hills and lakes, small farms, and country villages. The minister and writer Henry Ward Beecher was the first to suggest the similarity between this area and the English Lake District, the home of William Wordsworth, Samuel Taylor Coleridge, and Robert Southey, among others.[2] The comparison is an apt one, for not only are there many similarities between the landscapes of these two regions—both were also the homes of some of the nine-teenth century's greatest writers. The American Lake District (as the Stockbridge-Lenox region is called) was the home of Nathaniel Hawthorne, Herman Melville, William Cullen Bryant, James Russell Lowell, Oliver Wendell Holmes, and Henry Wadsworth Longfellow. William Ellery Channing and Ralph Waldo Emerson were frequent visitors. Other residents and visitors included Matthew Arnold, George William Curtis, James T. Fields,

Horace Greeley, Washington Irving, Fanny Kemble, Harriet Martineau, Harriet Beecher Stowe, and Nathaniel Parker Willis. During the years from 1840 to 1860, many of the more significant and popular American writers lived or visited in the Berkshires.

The social leader of the American Lake District was Catharine Maria Sedgwick. Her family moved to the Berkshires long before any other writer lived there, and the Sedgwicks were socially the most respected people in the region. At this time, Miss Sedgwick was considered by both critics and the public to be one of the country's major writers. Hawthorne believed that she was "our most truthful novelist," and for more than forty years critics and literary historians linked her with Bryant, Irving, and James Fenimore Cooper as one of the great founders of American literature.[3] Her fame and the fame of her novels, several of which were set in the Berkshires, first brought the Stockbridge-Lenox area to the attention of the public. According to the Cyclopedia of American Literature (1855) by Evert and George Duyckinck, the "wide-spread celebrity" of Stockbridge was "to be ascribed far more to the reputation which Miss Sedgwick's descriptions and works have given it, than to its great natural advantages."[4] Some forty years later, the Century Magazine ascribed the literati's love of the Berkshires to Miss Sedgwick's presence there; and an early guide to the area, The Berkshire Book, noted with approbation that Miss Sedgwick's home in Lenox "at once made the town known to all the reading, literary, and leading people of the day."[5] Between 1840 and 1860 literally dozens of American, English, and European authors visited her in the Berkshires where she maintained apartments both in the home of her brother Charles in Lenox and in the house in Stockbridge where she had been born. There were surely many aspiring writers who would have considered it a mark of distinction to secure an opportunity for tea with Miss Sedgwick in the Berkshires —for so had come Harriet Martineau from England, Fredrika Bremer from Sweden, William Gilmore Simms from the South, Washington Irving from New York, and William Ellery Channing from Boston.

II *A Record of Success*

Miss Sedgwick's respected position among the writers of the American Lake District was a culmination of one of the most successful literary careers in America up to that time. I do not mean to imply, however, that her career was successful solely in terms of the literary merits of her books; rather, I mean that her writings received a larger measure of favorable critical and popular attention than did the writings of many of her contemporaries. Indeed, until Harriet Beecher Stowe published *Uncle Tom's Cabin*, Miss Sedgwick was the *only* woman who was widely considered a major American writer. Her critics and the public were attracted to her indisputable faith in democracy, her liberal Protestantism, and her ideas on the place of women in American society. Her critics largely welcomed her opinions on various social, economic, political, and religious movements of the day; and they commented enthusiastically about her characterizations of New Englanders and about her ability to create credible portraits of Puritan Boston and New York during the Revolution.

One aspect of Miss Sedgwick's writings which certainly attracted readers was her willingness to satirize the social class into which she was born: the aristocracy of wealth. Through her mother's family, Miss Sedgwick was related to some of the wealthiest and socially influential Bostonians and New Yorkers. Long before she wrote her first book, she was acquainted with many of the country's most successful bankers, merchants, and lawyers. Indeed her father, a distinguished member of the Federalist party, was an outspoken advocate of allowing wealthy aristocrats to run the country—a sentiment which he shared with his good friend Alexander Hamilton. However, like her brothers, Miss Sedgwick was a faithful Jacksonian who believed in the common man and had little trust in the aristocracy of wealth. *Clarence* and *Married or Single?* are novels which satirize upper-class life, a subject which few American novelists have personally known as well as she did. The Sedgwicks' social position was of the greatest value in providing her with materials for her fiction.

Miss Sedgwick's religious views were as democratic as her political views, and she early rejected the pessimistic Calvinism of her ancestors in favor of the more liberal teachings of Unitarianism. Rather than accept the Calvinist picture of a merciless God who ruled men of essentially corrupt and sinful natures, she turned to Unitarianism; and its emphasis on the natural goodness of man marks all her writings. *The Linwoods* (1835)—which centers on the romance of a wealthy aristocrat and a poor Yankee— is clearly the work of a Jacksonian concerned with the plight of the common man; and *Hope Leslie* (1827), which is set in Puritan Massachusetts, offers a heroine who sees little but good in others and whose religious views are consequently closer to those of nineteenth-century Unitarians than those of seventeenth-century Calvinists.

Jacksonians and Unitarians had special reasons for applauding Miss Sedgwick's works; and, therefore, it should not surprise us that she was enthusiastically praised in those journals which shared her views. For example, *The North American Review* consistently praised her novels, and since this was the most scholarly and learned journal in the country, it was surely the right place to receive warm critical attention. It is very much to the point, however, to note that at this time, *The North American Review* was a bastion of the Unitarian faith.

Miss Sedgwick's works seemed especially significant to feminists since she had succeeded in a field traditionally dominated by men. Margaret Fuller devotes several paragraphs to her in *Women in the Nineteenth Century*. Miss Sedgwick is, she says, "a fine example of the independent and beneficent existence that intellect and character can give to Woman, no less than Man. . . ."[6] Although Miss Sedgwick was not actively a feminist, and although, as her didactic tales indicate, she clearly believed a woman's place was in the home, she did provide women characters who were more alive, more fully sketched out than the women in other American novels of the 1820's and 1830's. Although her women are notably dependent on men in most areas of social, political, and economic life, there are few of Cooper's two-dimensional "females" in her novels.

Furthermore, her heroines are all morally independent; as moral judges, that is, they defer to no one. In some instances, her heroines prove themselves as courageous as men; in *Hope Leslie,* for example, the Indian maiden Magawisca saves the life of Everell Fletcher even though it means risking her own life in order to do so. Miss Sedgwick offered the feminist not only the example of her own success but also a series of fictional portraits of women who were morally the equals of men and thoroughly as capable of the traditionally male virtues, bravery and courage.

Perhaps the main reason for Miss Sedgwick's popular and critical success was that she began to publish her novels at exactly that moment when Americans were most concerned about locating a native literature. In 1820, the English critic Sydney Smith asked his notorious question, "in the four quarters of the globe, who reads an American book?" Within a decade, Americans were able to list four authors whose works had been well received on both sides of the Atlantic: Bryant, Cooper, Irving, and Sedgwick. Cooper later offended his countrymen with his criticisms of American life, but the other three writers continued to be venerated because they had provided their country with a literature when national pride most required one. By 1850, it had become virtually a tradition to speak highly of Miss Sedgwick as well as Bryant and Irving, and her reviewers were generally capable of finding kind words with which to praise her literary efforts. It was with good reason that Washington Irving spoke of her "classic pen."[7]

Unitarians and other anti-Calvinists, Jacksonians, feminists, and Americans in general could all find something of interest in Miss Sedgwick's novels. Unlike such recent critics as Alexander Cowie and Michael Davitt Bell, her contemporaries were not troubled by the fact that some of her plot devices and characters were borrowed from conventional English and American romances.[8] Indeed, few readers found anything to criticize in her writings; and those few who did not like her works generally disagreed with her on political and religious grounds. On the other hand, Miss Sedgwick was always surprised by the great popularity of her writings; it was a popularity which she

neither sought nor expected? She held her abilities as a
writer in very low esteem; and, if her brothers had not
encouraged her to pursue a career as an author, it is likely
that she would never have written a book.

III   *River Gods and Mountain Gods*

In Miss Sedgwick's *Clarence* (1830), one female character states that her "family has always been in the very
first society, and it is natural that I should wish my children to associate with my relatives.[10] Within Miss Sedgwick's family there were women like this one. There was,
for example, her stepmother, Penelope Russell, a Boston
lady "of a highly-respectable family, an agreeable exterior,
and an attractive vivacity." She knew, however, nothing
of life in the country and was entirely out of place in the
Sedgwick home in Stockbridge. "She fluttered gracefully enough through the inanities of town drawing-rooms,"
Miss Sedgwick wrote, "but the reality and simplicity of
our country life was insupportable to her."[11]

As a child, however, Miss Sedgwick found country life
no less disagreeable than her stepmother did. "Stockbridge," she wrote her father in 1804, when she was
fifteen, "is barren of incidents to call forth either wonder,
admiration, or disgust. I sincerely believe there has nothing happened since your departure that has affected us as
much, or appeared of half the importance, as some wounds
which old Bose [the cow] has received."[12] Miss Sedgwick
was not the only one in her family, aside from her stepmother, who found the long months in Stockbridge somewhat boring. According to one observer, her sisters Elizabeth and Frances thought "Stockbridge the most intolerable
place in the world."[13] As a child, Miss Sedgwick was far
happier among her socially élite relatives in Boston and
New York than she was at the family homestead in Stockbridge.

Her mother's family was distinguished both socially
and politically. Through the family of her mother, Pamela
Dwight, Miss Sedgwick could trace her lineage to the aristocracy of the Connecticut River Valley—the members

of which were known as the "River Gods" because of the immense power they had over colonial affairs. When Miss Sedgwick's father Theodore announced his desire to marry Pamela Dwight, the "River Gods" were not at all pleased. "My mother's family," wrote Miss Sedgwick, "objected to my father on the score of family, they priding themselves on their gentle blood."[14] Theodore later became the leader of the "Mountain Gods," political leaders from the Berkshires with at least as much power as those from the Connecticut River Valley, but this development was in the future; and, as far as the "River God" families could see, the prospective husband was little more than an unaccomplished lawyer from the hills. Furthermore, Theodore could offer no "family"; indeed, much of his early life was spent in poverty. Nonetheless, the objections of Pamela's relatives were overcome, and on April 17, 1774, Theodore Sedgwick and Pamela Dwight were married.

Eleven years later, the Sedgwick mansion on the main street in Stockbridge was built. Throughout Miss Sedgwick's lifetime, it was one of the largest buildings in the town. The house and its setting appear in Miss Sedgwick's *A New-England Tale* as the home of the hero of that novel, Mr. Lloyd: "The house stood at a little distance from the road, more than half hid by two patriarchal elms. Behind the house, the grounds descended gradually to the Housatonick . . . . On the opposite side of the river, and from its very margin, rose a precipitous mountain, with its rich garniture of beach, maple, and linden; tree surmounting tree, and the images of all sent back by the clear mirror below; for the current there was so gentle, that, in the days of fable, a poet might have fancied the Genius of the stream had paused to woo the Nymphs of the wood."[15]

In this mansion on one of the coldest nights of the year 1789, three days after Christmas, Catharine Maria Sedgwick was born, the ninth child and fourth daughter of Theodore and Pamela. Of her brothers and sisters, three had died before her birth; and, with the exception of Charles, she was the youngest. As Miss Sedgwick wrote, she "was reared in an atmosphere of high intelligence. My father had uncommon mental vigor. So had my brothers. Their daily habits, and pursuits, and pleasures were intellectual, and I naturally imbibed from them a kindred taste."[16]

Miss Sedgwick's education followed lines dictated for a young lady of the day. She wrote that "no one dictated my studies or overlooked my progress," yet she did attend not only the local district schools but also select ones for young women.[17] By the time she was ten or twelve, she was reading a study of ancient history and less ponderous volumes as well, most of them forgotten today—Tom Brown's *Letters from the Dead to the Living* ("which had a strange charm for me") and Mrs. Anna Barbauld's *Economy of Human Life* ("very unmeaning and tedious"), among others.[18] As for the select schools she attended, in Albany there was Mrs. Bell's, "sustained by the first families in the land."[19] Later in Boston there was Mr. Payne's, which, Miss Sedgwick complained, taught her little French, although it left her much time to charm the Bostonians.

If her formal schooling left much to be desired, there was always her father, who "whenever he was at home, kept me up and at his side till nine o'clock in the evening, to listen to him while he read . . . Hume, or Shakespeare, or Don Quixote [sic], or Hudibras [sic]."[20] "I believe," she once wrote, "that the people who surround us in our childhood, whose atmosphere infolds us, as it were, have more to do with the formation of our characters than all our didactic and perceptive education."[21] She had, in short, the type of education that she later advocated in such books as *Home* (1835)—an education which owed less to the formalities of the schoolroom than to the intellectual environment of the home.

The literary education which her father provided was, of course, quite valuable to Miss Sedgwick as a writer. Of somewhat less value was the political education he tried to give her. Like Cooper, Irving, and Bryant, Miss Sedgwick could claim a strong Federalist background—one against which she, like the other three writers, in most respects rebelled. But, although she became a vehement Democrat, she absorbed much of her father's aristocratic attitude, a fact which explains the attitude which she herself took in many of her didactic tales. Alexander Cowie in *The Rise of the American Novel* refers to this attitude as one of the significant aspects of her fiction.[22] Miss Sedgwick always approached social problems from the secure heights of one born to an aristocracy, and there is evident condescension in her attitude toward the lower classes.

Miss Sedgwick's father had raised himself from a life of absolute poverty to one of considerable wealth and political influence. Writing to his eldest son in 1801, he remarked that "I remember how painful was my prospect when I was making my entry into life, without friends from whom I could expect anything, without any property, young, and with a most diffident opinion of my own talents the prospect exhibited a settled gloom. I did all but dispair [sic]. To this I did not submit. On the contrary, I determined, if possible, to succeed & I did succeed."[23]

Theodore Sedgwick had been born near Hartford in 1746; but, while he was still young, his family had moved to the small farming community of Cornwall, Connecticut, where his father died in 1757. To keep the family together, Theodore's brother John ran a tavern in the village; and part of his earnings sent Theodore to Yale, from which he was expelled for reasons long forgotten. For a while he studied to be a minister but, with the blessings of his tutor, changed to law and became a student under his cousin, Colonel Mark Hopkins. In 1766, Theodore was admitted to the bar; and he opened a practice in Great Barrington, Massachusetts, just south of Stockbridge. But, Miss Sedgwick wrote, "for six weeks he sat looking up and down the street . . . for a client, but no client came, and he took down his sign and moved off to Sheffield [Massachusetts], where he began his honorable legal career."[24]

Theodore Sedgwick played an active role in the Revolutionary War and was a member of the Provincial Congress. He early made known his desire for a strong central government and was active in suppressing Shays' Rebellion. (His part in the suppression of the rebellion is central to Edward Bellamy's novel *The Duke of Stockbridge*.) Not surprisingly,

Miss Sedgwick, who always noted her father's deeds with care, appended a large footnote on the rebellion to *A New-England Tale*, her first book—though its relevance to that tale is something of a moot point.

The friend of George Washington, John Jay, Henry Knox, and Alexander Hamilton, Sedgwick was repeatedly a member of the United States Senate or the House during the nation's early years. He was a leader in the fight to gain ratification of the Federal Constitution, and he became one of the most prominent members of the Federalist government, a prominence which reached its height when he was chosen the Speaker of the United States House of Representatives. He once wrote that he considered himself "what is called a prosperous man. I have reason to bless God I have been less unfortunate, even in my own opinion, than many others."[25]

According to his biographer Richard E. Welch, Jr., Sedgwick's "political desires and philosophy . . . were almost identical" with Hamilton's.[26] He was as thoroughly aristocratic as any American of his day, and he regarded the mass of men as no better than "the 'greasy, unwashen multitude' of Rome."[27] Nor was he always friendly with his constituents. Miss Sedgwick remembered having "seen his brow lower when a free-and-easy mechanic came to the *front* door, and upon one occasion . . . turning off the 'east steps' (I am *sure* not kicking, but the demonstration was unequivocal) a grown-up lad who kept his hat on after being told to take it off."[28] He was no more able to tolerate the equalitarian thinking of Thomas Jefferson than he was able to tolerate disrespectful representatives of the lower orders. "In all the private relations of society he is an excellent man," wrote one visiting European nobleman, the Duke de La Rochefoucauld-Liancourt; but "in his politics he is somewhat warm, and not a little intolerant."[29]

In fact, Sedgwick seldom tolerated opinions which conflicted with his own; and he was unable to entertain new ideas—unless they had Federalist sanction or that of the Constitution; and he was destined, therefore, to fall with his political associates. After the rise to power of the Jeffersonians in 1800, he found himself increasingly unwelcome in the centers of government. He called Jefferson "the greatest rascal and traitor in the United States" and said of another politician that he was thought to be "a Federalist, but he is a fool, so he must be a Democrat."[30] The final blow against Sedgwick's career came in 1806 when, under the new regime, he was passed over as the choice for the Chief Justice of Massachusetts. "My friends try in vain to soothe me," he reported. "They say I am reconciled. . . . they lie like hell."[31]

Sedgwick's authoritarian and arrogant personality makes him seem a most disagreeable figure today, and yet there was another side to the man which also deserves attention: he was one of the first Americans to question the right to own slaves, and through his efforts slavery was abolished in Massachusetts. Sedgwick's most important contribution to the abolition of slavery in this state involved his legal defense of Elizabeth Freeman (or "Mumbet," as she was generally called), a slave belonging to Colonel John Ashley in Sheffield, Massachusetts. One day after she had been struck violently with a shovel by Ashley's wife, she sought protection from Theodore Sedgwick. The situation was a particularly difficult one for him, since Ashley was both a relative and a man of considerable political influence in Western Massachusetts. Moreover, he had long been among Sedgwick's closest friends. Placing, however, moral right above other considerations, Sedgwick was able to have "Mumbet" freed by using the recently established Massachusetts Declaration of Rights and the fact that in this state "slavery had never received specific legal sanction."[32] In appreciation, "Mumbet" became the devoted, life-long servant of the Sedgwick household; indeed, Miss Sedgwick was closer to her than she was to her own mother. "Mumbet had a clear and nice perception of justice," she wrote, "and a stern love of it, an uncompromising honesty in word and deed, and conduct of high intelligence, that made her the unconscious moral teacher of the children she tenderly nursed."[33] And she added, "In my childhood I clung to her with instinctive love and faith."[34]

Theodore Sedgwick was involved in other efforts to free slaves, notably in another law case, Greenwood vs. Curtis (1810) and in his membership in the Abolition

Society of Pennsylvania. But Sedgwick was not a radical, and he once declared in Congress that "to propose an abolition of slavery in this country would be the height of madness."[35] Furthermore, he was largely responsible for the first Fugitive Slave Law (1791), which he thought was essential for the well-being of the South and hence of the rest of the country as well.

Theodore's Abolitionism had a considerable effect on his children and especially his daughter. Both his sons Henry (in *The Practicability of the Abolition of Slavery*, 1831) and Theodore, Jr. (in *Public and Private Economy*, 1836) gave much attention to the subject. Miss Sedgwick was devoted to the Abolitionist cause, although not so actively as reformers like Lydia Maria Child and Harriet Beecher Stowe. Slavery is discussed in some of her novels, including *Redwood* which portrays an Uncle Tom thirty years before the publication of Mrs. Stowe's novel.

IV *Converting the Heathen*

Just as Miss Sedgwick was able to overcome her Federalist background, so was she able to overcome her religious training as a Calvinist. Among Miss Sedgwick's ancestors were several Calvinist ministers, and the area in which she lived had long been under the religious control of Calvinist missionaries and thinkers. One of the earliest white settlers was in fact Jonathan Edwards, who arrived in 1751 as a missionary to the Housatonic Indians. Edwards, incidentally, was not a very successful missionary; first of all, he was unable to speak the Housatonic language; and, second, he appeared less interested in mastering it than in completing *Freedom of Will*.

Edwards' successor was the Reverend Stephen West, who arrived in 1759 and who was the Stockbridge minister until 1819. In personality, he was a rather inoffensive, mild-mannered gentleman who had fallen, however, under the influence of one of Edwards' disciples, the self-righteous Samuel Hopkins from the neighboring town of Great Barrington—the same Samuel Hopkins who developed the theological system known, appropriately, as Hopkinsianism, one of the last bulwarks of Calvinism in New England.

(Hopkins, by the way, is the title figure in Harriet Beecher Stowe's *The Minister's Wooing*, where he is exhibited as the last thinker in the traditions of New England theology.)

The Reverend West was a powerful figure in the town during Miss Sedgwick's childhood. New England towns at this time still centered around their churches, and West was an especially demanding Calvinist. His influence no doubt caused Miss Sedgwick to spend much time in contemplating the nature of original sin; not until she joined the Unitarian Church in 1819 did she entirely overcome West's influence. It may be of interest here to note that her first book, *A New-England Tale,* was written as a response to her conversion to Unitarianism. The book was originally to have been a tract setting forth the doctrines of her new belief; in the process of writing, she expanded her subject to cover much more than simply the teachings of the Unitarian Church.

The Sedgwicks thought that West was personally a kind man, as the many references to him in Miss Sedgwick's letters testify; but they found little in either his sermons or his letters with which they could agree entirely. All of the Sedgwicks gave much thought to what he had to say—indeed, Miss Sedgwick later felt they had taken his Calvinism somewhat too seriously—but, except for Elizabeth, the oldest Sedgwick daughter, the only member of the family to join the Stockbridge church during his tenancy was their mother; and she really had little choice in the matter since she was his niece. It would not have said much for West's abilities as a preacher if a close relative like Mrs. Sedgwick had not joined. Miss Sedgwick was not able to extricate herself entirely from West's Calvinism until she joined the Unitarian Church when she was thirty. "The good little polemic," as she called the Reverend West, clearly had a substantial effect on her early religious development.[36]

V "That . . . Sacred Mansion"

Before Miss Sedgwick published her first novel, she had reformed both her political and her religious attitudes. She was no longer a Federalist, but a Democrat—no longer a Calvinist, but a Unitarian. Indeed, one of her (perhaps unconscious) objectives in her historical novels seems to have been a revision of the past; thus, in *The Linwoods* (1835), which deals with the American Revolution, there are many figures who historically became prominent Federalists, but there are few intimations of Federalist doctrine in the book.

Redwood, Clarence, and other novels by Miss Sedgwick which glorify domestic life and life in the country also involve a revision of the past—in this case, Miss Sedgwick's own. Her home life there was not always as pleasant as later she sometimes said it was. Her mother was described as possessing "a charming face and an air of refinement and elegance" in the redoubtable Mrs. E.F. Ellet's *Queens of American Society* and in her *Court Circles of the Republic,* yet her private life was quite different from anything Mrs. Ellet described.[37] Several times during Miss Sedgwick's childhood, her mother suffered long periods of mental depression. In Miss Sedgwick's autobiography, she described her mother's condition and suggested her own fears about that state of extreme depression which affected many members of her family:

My mother may have had a constitutional tendency to insanity, but I believe the delicate construction of a sensitive and reserved temperament, a constitution originally fragile, and roughly handled by the medical treatment of the times, and the terrible weight of domestic cares, will sufficiently account for her mental illness without supposing a cerebral tendency which her descendents may have inherited. But this fear may be wholesome to them, if it lead them to a careful physical training, to guarding against nervous susceptibilities and weakness, and to avoiding the stimulants and excitements so unfavorable to nervous constitutions. I firmly believe that people may be educated out of a hereditary tendency to insanity more surely than one can eradicate a liability to consumption, or any other scrofulous poison.[38]

But her family could well have found sufficient reason to fear "a hereditary tendency to insanity." There were several cases of insanity in her mother's family; Miss Sedgwick herself suffered extensive periods of depression, as did both her sisters; a nephew committed suicide; and her brother Henry died hopelessly insane.

Miss Sedgwick's childhood was by no means an ideal one. Not only was her mother much of the time in a state of extreme depression, but her father was away for months at a time. Once when he was in Philadelphia, Mrs. Sedgwick wrote to him, "I grant that the 'call of our country,' 'the voice of Fame,' and 'the Hon'ble,' 'right Hon'ble,' are high-sounding words. 'They play about the head, but come not near the heart.' A wish to serve the true interests of our country is certainly a laudable ambition, but the intention brings many cares with it."[39] While there is no question that Sedgwick was devoted to his wife and family, it is evident that he thought that his affairs in government and law were of greater importance. He never left politics for any length of time; rather, said Miss Sedgwick, he believed that it was "his duty to remain in public life at every private sacrifice."[40] Meanwhile, Mrs. Sedgwick's condition became progressively worse until her final and most severe attack in 1804. From this time until her death three years later, she remained a semi-invalid.

The year after Mrs. Sedgwick's death, her husband remarried. His new wife, Penelope Russell, was a lady of impeccable manners. However, as noted above, she found little use for her social graces in Stockbridge; and the Sedgwick home was surely no happier under her rule than it had been under her predecessor's. As soon after Theodore Sedgwick's death in 1812 as she deemed proper, she packed her bags and returned to the social life of her family home in Boston.

Miss Sedgwick's childhood was somewhat less happy than she later remembered. In her childhood, she had wished for extended visits to Boston and New York; later it seemed as if nothing could be better than a lifetime in the Berkshires. Four years after her father's death, she wrote to one of her sisters, "I look forward to a very happy summer at S[tockbridge]. Have we not always been happy there?"[41] Three years later, she told her brother Robert that "I sometimes think my love for that spot is for these philosophic, enlightened times, too much like that of the savage, who thinks his heaven is to be one great hunting-ground. There I have located my heaven."[42] And less than four years after this statement, her enthusiasm reached its greatest heights of exaggerated sentimentality: in Stock-bridge, "love and joy, and peace and praise are the spon-taneous language of the heart, and all in sweet accord with the voice that cometh from the mountains and the meadows, the waving branches and the frolic shadows."[43] Nostalgia had hidden reality from view. "Oh, what is good," wrote one of Miss Sedgwick's brothers to her, "if it be not to dwell upon all we have loved, and to cherish all we still love, in that, to me, sacred mansion!"[44] Indeed, the Sedgwick home was sacred to Theodore's children; and throughout their lives, they visited there as often as possi-ble. Miss Sedgwick spent more of her adult life there than anywhere else, and all her brothers spent many summer months and holidays there. Officially, it became the home of the senior brother, Theodore, Jr., but all the brothers and sisters considered it equally theirs.

Miss Sedgwick's close friendships with her brothers and sisters had a significant effect on her work. Not only do these close ties help explain the great emphasis given to family life in her works—but they also help to explain her politics, which she borrowed directly from her brothers, all of whom were Jacksonian Democrats. She herself knew little of politics and economics; what she did know of these subjects she learned from her brothers and from their books such as Theodore's *Public and Private Economy.*

Theodore (b. 1780), Miss Sedgwick's oldest brother, was a lawyer and the Massachusetts Democratic party's perennially defeated candidate for senator and for gover-nor. His books included *Hints to My Countrymen* (1826) and three volumes of *Public and Private Economy* (1836). He married Susan Anne Livingston Ridley, one of Miss Sedg-wick's closest friends and the author of numerous children's books, including *Allen Prescott* (1834) and *The Young Emigrants* (1836). These were didactic tales of the sort Miss Sedgwick began writing in the 1830's.

Miss Sedgwick's second brother, Henry (b. 1785), was the husband of Jane Minot of Boston, the daughter of the early American historian George Richards Minot. Henry is most famous for his attempts to simplify various American legal procedures, but he was also active in Abolitionist activities and in various other causes. His younger brother Robert (b. 1787) was his law partner in New York. Robert's wife was the cousin of William Ellery Channing, and through this family relationship Miss Sedgwick remained in close contact with the most famous of American Unitarians.

Miss Sedgwick's youngest brother, Charles (b. 1791), was a clerk of the Massachusetts Supreme Court. His wife, Elizabeth Buckminster Dwight, the granddaughter of Jonathan Edwards, was the author of children's books and the headmistress of a school for young ladies. Charles and his wife lived in Lenox, and Miss Sedgwick maintained an apartment in one wing of their house.

Miss Sedgwick also had two sisters, Elizabeth (b. 1775) and Frances (b. 1778). Both sisters married distinguished gentlemen: Elizabeth married Thaddeus Pomeroy, a lawyer in Stockbridge; Frances, Ebenezer Watson, a senior partner in the New York publishing firm of Whiting and Watson. Both sisters, incidentally, suffered, like Miss Sedgwick and their mother, from protracted periods of melancholy.

VI A Society of Women

By the time she was twenty-six, Miss Sedgwick was already speaking of herself as a spinster; and she stated her chief business in life was to care for the family home and for the comforts of her brothers and sisters. For the rest of her life, she remained close to members of her family. Indeed, most of her adult years were spent in her brothers' homes. Her closest friends included two of her sisters-in-law, Susan Anne Sedgwick and Elizabeth Dwight Sedgwick. Together with the Shakespearean actress Fanny Kemble, these three Sedgwick women formed the "inner circle" of Berkshire society. While members of the American Lake District provided Miss Sedgwick with a large number of friends who shared her literary interests, she spent most of her time with this "inner circle" and with her brothers and sisters.

The Swedish novelist Fredrika Bremer noted the lack of

men in Miss Sedgwick's "inner circle." "The country around
Lenox is romantically lovely," she wrote.

Amid this scenery have Catharine Sedgwick and Nathaniel
Hawthorne their rural homes. I had been invited to both, and I
wished to see both. I spent four-and-twenty hours with the
excellent and amiable Catharine Sedgwick and her family, en-
joying her company and that of several agreeable ladies. There
were no gentlemen—gentlemen, indeed, seemed to be rare
in social circles of this neighborhood. But they were less missed
here than is generally the case in society, because the women
of this little circle are possessed of unusual intellectual cultivation—several of them endowed with genius and talents of a high
order. Fanny Kemble has her home here when she resides
in America. . . . The scenery is beautiful; these ladies enjoy
it and each other's society, and life lacks nothing to the greater
number.[45]

In the early 1850's, the time of which Miss Bremer was
writing, Lenox and its surrounding communities included
Hawthorne, Melville, Holmes, and many other writers
among the summer and year-round residents, yet as Miss
Bremer's account suggests, the male segment of the American Lake District had little contact with Miss Sedgwick's
"inner circle." The Sedgwick group was not entirely
isolated, however, from the male writers who were living
in the region; and the most common meeting ground
appears to have been the Sedgwick homes in Stockbridge
and Lenox. The Sedgwick soirées brought members of the
American Lake District together to hear Fanny Kemble
sing ballads or recite passages from Shakespeare; and—
with the notable exceptions of Thoreau, Whitman, and
Poe—virtually every American author of note attended
afternoon tea with Miss Sedgwick.

The most famous of these teas occurred on August 5, 1850,
and included Melville, Hawthorne, Holmes, the novelist
Cornelius Mathews, the publisher James T. Fields, the
lawyer David Dudley Field, and the editor George Duyckinck as well as Miss Sedgwick. What is usually remembered about this particular Berkshire day is that it provided
Melville's first introduction to Hawthorne, and hence

began one of the most significant friendships in American literary history.[46] The day's adventures had apparently been planned as something of a light-hearted homage to the senior members of the American Lake District, Miss Sedgwick and William Cullen Bryant. In the morning the group climbed Monument Mountain, located at the other end of the meadows south of the Sedgwick family home and at the summit, Mathews read Bryant's "Monument Mountain."

In the afternoon, Melville, Hawthorne, Holmes, Fields, Duyckinck, and various others, including the historian and biographer Joel Tyler Headley, were led through Stockbridge's "Ice Glen," one of the settings in Miss Sedgwick's first novel, *A New-England Tale*. Earlier in the day some of the group had climbed up a hill to "sacrifice rock," the setting for an episode in *Hope Leslie*. The day concluded with a tea at the Field home, followed by, as Evert Duyckinck reported to his wife, "a cross examination . . . on Hope Leslie and Magawisca," the Indian maiden who very nearly loses her life at "sacrifice rock" in *Hope Leslie*.[47]

The events of August 5, 1850, were unique in the history of the American Lake District; but there are other accounts of Sedgwick teas and soirées at which she welcomed the best known of American authors.[48] However, it remains clear that Miss Sedgwick continued to restrict her circle of intimate acquaintances to her sisters-in-law and Fanny Kemble. She had much in common with Susan and Elizabeth Sedgwick; for, like her, they had obtained both popular and critical success as the authors of didactic tales. And Fanny Kemble, the greatest Shakespearean actress of her day, had proven Miss Sedgwick's thesis that women could succeed as well as men—a thesis which was not accepted, of course, by many of her contemporaries. Kemble, wrote Miss Sedgwick, was "steeped to the very lips in genius."[49]

VII *New York*

Commentators on Miss Sedgwick's life and critics of her works have traditionally associated her with the hill towns of Berkshire County; but, while it was here that she "located [her] heaven," she spent a few months each year in New

York and visited extensively in Boston. Her father's position as Speaker of the United States House of Representatives assured the Sedgwick family of a place in the "Court Circles of the Republic," as Mrs. E.F. Ellet called the upper-crust society of the early nation. Furthermore, Miss Sedgwick's mother was related to many socially prominent Boston and New York families. In her girlhood, she moved gracefully through this society and, at the age of nineteen, was described by her brother Henry as "a little thing in petticoats . . pretty, amiable, and accomplished."[50]

Later, in the 1820's and 1830's she spent much time at the New York townhouses of her brothers Henry and Robert where the society was marked less by family relationships than by artistic and literary interests. William Cullen Bryant, who was encouraged by the Sedgwick brothers to move to New York to join their law firm, has left a record of the society which met at their homes. The poet Robert Sands and the author and statesman Gulian C. Verplanck were frequent visitors. Other visitors at the Sedgwick homes included the poets James Hillhouse and Fitz-Greene Halleck, "then in the height of his poetical reputation." James Fenimore Cooper was seen often at the Sedgwick homes, but he later argued with Robert and so broke off "his intimacy with the family." Other guests included the New York wit Anthony Bleeker and the artists Samuel F.B. Morse, who later perfected the telegraph, and Thomas Cole, who is considered the founder of the Hudson River School of painting.[51]

The type of society which met at her brothers' homes was much different from the society, founded solely on wealth and genealogy, which Miss Sedgwick had known from childhood and which she mercilessly satirized in *Clarence* and in *Married or Single?* Miss Sedgwick inherited both money (from her father) and ancestors (from her mother); but, while her wealth left her free to write—and to travel extensively—and while her mother's family insured her a place in New York and Boston society, she considered virtue and talent to be qualitites of the greatest significance. While in New York, she once wrote to a niece that she had found time to meet Angelina and Sarah

Moore Grimké, Abolitionist sisters from South Carolina, but not the time to visit one society matron full of "all the pride of rank" or another at whose home "there still survives a certain elegance, and all the stiffness of a *société choisie.*"[52]

VIII *Borrowings for Fiction*

Miss Sedgwick employed her knowledge of New York and particularly its aristocracy of birth and wealth in *Clarence* and *Home,* among other didactic tales, where American urban life is contrasted with life in the country, but in general, she wrote only about the country. *A New-England Tale,* for example, is clearly set in the Stockbridge of her girlhood; and *Redwood* deals with rural New England of the 1820's. Furthermore, in at least two books, *A New-England Tale* and *Home,* she used her family home as one of the settings. Even her historical novels employed settings which she knew well—indeed, the Indian encampment in *Hope Leslie* is situated on the Great Meadow south of Stockbridge—and her accounts of Puritan life and the Revolutionary War include, as we will see, information which had been handed down in her family. Above all, Miss Sedgwick incorporated her own strong sense of family life in her works, especially in her didactic tales. Her fiction was very largely built from her own experiences, and the autobiographical aspects of her works are underscored in the chapters which follow.

CHAPTER 2

Geneva and the Berkshire Hills

[The Yankee's] religion is praktikal; he mourns over the heathen, and iz reddy tew save them by the job.

—Josh Billings[1]

Flat roof, tall steeple,
Blind guide, ignorant people.

—Nathan Torrey[2]

I *Getting to Heaven*

THESE two Berkshirites, Josh Billings and Nathan Torrey, were not alone in believing that the religion of their community was somehow lacking. Among Miss Sedgwick's closer friends was the Reverend Orville Dewey, a once-noted Unitarian minister whose childhood had been spent in the Berkshire village of Sheffield. Writing of the days when he was growing up, Dewey stated that in his area there was "a great deal of dissent expressed from the popular theology. . . . It was a frequent topic in our house, especially after a sermon on the decrees, or election, or the sinner's total inability to comply with the conditions on which salvation was offered to him. The dislike of these doctrines increased and spread here, till it became a revolt of nearly half the town against them."[3]

In addition to Dewey, we have the comments of Timothy Dwight, president of Yale, who wrote of the Great Barrington of the early 1800's that here, where the Reverend Samuel Hopkins had once held court, "religion has had. . . . , generally, a doubtful existence; and, during the little time in which they have had a minister of the Gospel, he has scarcely been able to find a subsistence."[4] Finally, we have the interesting comment made in 1829 by Stockbridge's own Reverend David Dudley Field in his *History of Berkshire County*. Field had to be somewhat biased in his observations, for, should it appear that religion in his area was not accepted, was it not at least in part the fault of his evangelical powers? Nonetheless, he had to admit, even if it was an understatement of the case, that in the Berkshires "individuals may be found . . . who do nothing for the support of the gospel." He added that, in such cases, "public worship has . . . been gradually forsaken, and finally abandoned; and their children, in many instances, have grown up in ignorance and sin."[5]

While it may at times seem as if Frances Trollope was not far from the truth when she proclaimed that "all the bigotry in America was concentrated upon the Berkshire Hills," it should be obvious by now that, if the Sedgwicks were among the most outspoken, they were not the county's only liberal infidels.[6] Long before the appearance of *A New-England Tale*, a revolt against the established religion—and, in Massachusetts, Congregationalism was the politically sanctioned faith until 1833—had been increasing its number of "converts" in the Berkshires as well as in the rest of the state. "The country," Miss Sedgwick indignantly proclaimed, "is condemned to the ministration of inferior men."[7]

Leading the opposition, at the time of the publication of *A New-England Tale*, was the spirit of the late Reverend Samuel Hopkins, a student of Jonathan Edwards and the author of the characteristically titled volume *Sin: An Advantage to the Universe*. From his Great Barrington pulpit, Hopkins had expounded a theology which had its effect not only on his community and the rest of the Berkshires but also on Calvinist thought in America. He is still notorious for his belief that a true Christian must be willing to be damned eternally if this will glorify God. Although a remarkably uninspiring preacher, his emphasis on immediate conversion—and, thereby, revivalism—produced an effect felt from the crossroad towns of Berkshire to the backwoods of Kentucky and the farthest reaches of the American frontier.

One of Hopkins' students was the Reverend Stephen
West, a man for whom Miss Sedgwick as a child had very
little respect. "I dreaded him," she wrote, "and certainly
did not understand him in my youth. He was then only the
dry, sapless embodiment of polemical divinity."[8] Theologically, however, West was as concerned with the Atonement as
with eternal damnation. "If such ineffable divine tenderness," he wrote in one of his books, "appeared in God's
treatment of his offending offspring in the first opening
of a scheme of mercy, and of redemption by Christ; what a
majesty and glory of Love will shine forth in its comple-
tion!"[9] Nonetheless, the emphasis he gives elsewhere to
revivalism—and to sin and repentance—accounts for the attitude taken by Miss Sedgwick and others during their
childhood toward a man who was really quite genial and
mild in manner.

But geniality and mildness were not enough to keep
Doctor West's expressed doctrines from leading in the
presumably Christian hill towns to such predictable characteristics as overenthusiasm, intolerance, and hypocrisy.
Especially amusing in the history of the Stockbridge
church is the case involving those members who decided
in 1812 to form a Society for the Preservation of Christian
Morals. According to one historian, the members of this
group "took their turns in spending the Sabbath at the ho-
tel to stop travellers, hand bills were circulated, and efforts
were made to purify the sacred enclosure of the church"
from the sins of "Intemperance, Sabbath-breaking, and Profanity."[10] Such naïve enthusiasm—since the members of
the society necessarily were absent from church and, therefore, were Sabbath-breaking themselves—would have been
perfectly harmless, of course, had it remained on this level;
but, unfortunately, as Doctor West discovered, only one
step existed between this enthusiasm and intolerance. For
example, the Widow Ingersoll, whose husband had been
a deacon in Doctor West's church, rented her husband's
hat shop to Billy Brogan, an Irish Catholic. There was at
this time no Catholic Church in the vicinity of Stockbridge,
but the local Catholics decided to invite a priest to perform mass in the town; and, since the hat shop was the

largest place available, it seemed the best place for the mass to be celebrated. The intolerant Mrs. Ingersoll was horrified at the idea, and she soon informed Mr. Brogan that she would rather burn the building than allow it to be used for Catholic rituals. Indignantly, she made it known that she had rented Mr. Brogan a hat shop, not a cathedral![11]

If, on the one hand, Stockbridge and the rest of the Berkshire hilltowns had many residents like the Widow Ingersoll—people, that is, who were intolerant of all religious beliefs except their own—there were, on the other hand, such people as Orville Dewey, who broke away from Calvinism and became the associate of William Ellery Channing and the friend of Ralph Waldo Emerson—whom he addressed as "Dear Waldo."[12] Dewey became a Unitarian; and, like Channing and Emerson, he rejected the doctrine of original sin—the doctrine which insists that all men are fundamentally evil. Furthermore, he refused to accept the Calvinist belief in predestination—the belief, that is, that at the beginning of time, God decided who would be damned and who would be saved. As a Unitarian, Dewey believed that salvation was available to all people and that all people were fundamentally good. Furthermore, he insisted on a toleration of all religious practices. In 1819, Unitarian doctrines were codified by William Ellery Channing; and two years later, Miss Sedgwick joined the growing number of Berkshire residents who had left Calvinism to become Unitarians. It is worth noting, however, that there were not enough Unitarians in Stockbridge to support their own church; the Calvinists continued to predominate.

Miss Sedgwick believed that Doctor West's Calvinistic preachings were responsible in large part for the long periods of melancholia which her sister Elizabeth suffered. "She was so true, so practical," wrote Miss Sedgwick; ". . . she believed . . . [the] monstrous doctrines [of Calvinism], and they made her gloomy."[13] Nor was Elizabeth the only member of the Sedgwick family on whom Doctor West's theology had less than a healthy effect. "I do, my dear Frances," wrote Miss Sedgwick to her sister in 1810, feel my utter destitution of any "claim to reward," my entire helplessness as it regards any merit of my own, and entire dependence on mercy, mediation, and atonement. . . . I am utterly destitute of those holy affections which should be so completely incorporated with our being as to become a part of it. . . . There have been moments of my life when I have had a lively, importunate, though, alas! transient interest awakened in serious things, but the cares and the pleasures of this world have operated on these sudden impulses as the "thorns" in the parable. Change of scene or society has induced me to shake off these impressions as fetters that constrained my vivacity, and to venture forward again, forgetful of the precious anchor I had so lightly thrown away.[14]

About the time of this letter Miss Sedgwick joined the church of a Doctor Mason in New York. Mason was a Calvinist who spent much time assuring his parishioners that they were essentially sinful people; indeed, he once went so far as to tell them that "they had fellowship with the devil; no, he would not slander the devil, they were worse."[15] Miss Sedgwick later broke from Mason's church, but the genius of Geneva had left his stamp on the future author; and, while her books contain a fair proportion of angels, they also contain dark, unredeemable fiends who would undoubtedly have been intriguing subjects for dissection by Samuel Hopkins and his theological descendants.

II *The Infidel of Stockbridge*

In January, 1813, the Honorable Theodore Sedgwick, to the surprise of various Stockbridge residents, made a deathbed conversion before none other than the Reverend William Ellery Channing. When "Mr. Channing visited papa," Miss Sedgwick wrote to one of her sisters,

Papa imparted to him his earnest desire to unite himself to the visible Church, and his reluctance to defer it. Mr. C., who indeed is a minister of consolation from the throne of mercy, readily acquiesced in his wishes. He explained to him his understanding of this holy sacrament, which agreed entirely with papa's. He then proceeded to administer it in the most solemn and affecting manner. Papa expressed, in receiving it, his desire to repose himself entirely on the merits and atonement of our

Savior. The performance of this duty seemed to remove the bar of reserve that opposed the flowing out of papa's heart, and he now shows that he feels his tenure of life to be very slight, and that his affections dwell on heavenly things.[16]

After her father's death, Miss Sedgwick remained in contact with the Channings. In 1821 Miss Sedgwick decided to become a member of the Unitarian Society in New York; and, to some, her decision was a resounding shock. Certain residents of Stockbridge were stunned, and some of the "River Gods" must have concluded that, in the end, little good had come of allowing their Pamela to unite with a Sedgwick. "Come and see me as often as you can, dear," a favorite aunt told Miss Sedgwick, "for you know, after this world, we shall never meet again."[17]

Meanwhile, however, the newly arrived Stockbridge minister, the Reverend David Dudley Field, pointed with pride to his most recent revival; if one had escaped from the fold, he could note nonetheless that in Stockbridge alone ninety-four had been added to the membership. In the Berkshires, the influence of Samuel Hopkins was as strong as ever. About the same time, Miss Sedgwick's brother Theodore began encouraging her to write a book. Although she at first called this "a most extravagant estimate of my powers," she decided the following year to declare her religious stand by writing a tale in the form of a tract. Having completed it, she showed the work to her brother Henry, who was sufficiently impressed with it to encourage her to develop it into a novel. The expanded work, *A New-England Tale; or, Sketches of New-England Character and Manners*, was published in the spring of 1822.[18]

III   *A Viper from the Hills*

A New-England Tale is the story of an orphan named Jane Elton left in the care of her aunt, Mrs. Wilson, who can see little good in the character of her young niece. Mrs. Wilson constantly upbraids the girl for presumed shortcomings, but at the same time she praises Davis and Elvira, her own children, who are later shown to be both corrupt and vicious. Meanwhile, Jane finds sympathetic understanding in a good Quaker named Mr. Lloyd, whom she marries at the end of the novel. The story has obvious affinities with the Cinderella legend—although in this case the "prince" is a Quaker—but Miss Sedgwick has taken the legend and has adapted it carefully to a New England setting of the early nineteenth century.

Jane Elton is the daughter of a proud, once wealthy merchant who has made some unfortunate speculations and thereby reduced his family to near poverty. Jane's mother, on the other hand, "never seemed elated by prosperity"; and therefore, she serves as a contrast to her husband, who has reduced the wealth of his family in his greed for more money.[19] The family servant Mary Hull, like the Sedgwicks' own servant "Mumbet," is "endowed with a mind of uncommon strength, and an affectionate heart"; and she, the reader is told, has played a large role in the formation of Jane's character. Thus Jane is essentially a charitable girl with the mental strength to resist the corruptions of the world outside her family. Miss Sedgwick believed that all people are essentially good but that the world may corrupt them unless their characters are sufficiently strong to resist this corruption.

When Jane is twelve, both parents die, and she is immediately exposed to a world which is indifferent to her emotions. At the funeral for her mother, for example, the minister reminds his congregation not of salvation but of the biblical statement "the wages of sin is death."[20] Jane is left to the mercy of her father's three sisters, Mrs. Daggett, Mrs. Convers, and Mrs. Wilson. Rather than comfort their niece and assure her that someone will provide her with a new home, the three women make it clear that they have no desire to adopt Jane. Only after much discussion does Mrs. Wilson agree to adopt her.[21]

Mrs. Wilson is one of the strongest pillars of the church in her village (which, incidentally, is similar to Stockbridge, although no direct reference is made to the fact). Mrs. Wilson, says Miss Sedgwick, "fancied herself one of the subjects of an awakening at an early period of her life; had passed through the ordeal of a church-examination with great credit," but, adds the author, "we fear that in those times of excitement, during which many pass from indifference to holiness, and many are converted from sin to righteousness, there are also many who, like Mrs. Wilson, delude themselves and others with vain forms of words and professions of faith."[22] On this basis the author launches her attack on the religious hypocrisy of her presumably pious Stockbridge neighbors. Mrs. Wilson professes to believe in saving through faith, which, as the author spares no words in demonstrating, is a very convenient thing for those who have no good works to offer. Meanwhile, a Quaker named Lloyd arrives in town and hires Mary Hull as his servant. He also begins to take an interest in Jane Elton, who, as we are always reminded, is heroically enduring much.

In the Wilson household, there are about a half-dozen children—exactly how many never becomes clear—but only two of them, Elvira and David, are of any real importance to the tale. Elvira tells the Christian Jane that "you have brought your deaconish nonsense to a poor market. It was easy enough to get along with the truth with your mother, because she would let you have your own way on all occasions; but I tell you, disguises are the only wear in our camp!"[23]

Meanwhile, plans are made for a dancing school in the county; and, since this is the New England of the early nineteenth century, the "Godly" find the plans to be beyond endurance: "Some clergymen denounced the impending sin from their pulpits. One said that he had searched the Bible from Genesis to Revelation, and he could not find a text that expressly treated of that enormity, but that was manifestly because it was a sin too heinous to be spoken of in holy writ.[24]" Mrs. Wilson claims, of course, that she is in full agreement with the local divines; and she sees to it that the town's church establishes two more weekly meetings, timed to concur with the meetings of the dancing school; Elvira, of course, must attend the church.

However, Elvira has constructed a plan whereby she can fool her mother and go to the dance with Edward

Erskine, who, Miss Sedgwick makes clear, is as morally corrupt as the Wilson children. Elvira's plan is exposed in such a way as to make it seem that Jane is really the guilty party. Although, characteristically, Jane had been nursing a dying servant at the time, she meekly endures the false accusation. In the end, Elvira runs away with a disreputable Frenchman,—an opportunity for Miss Sedgwick to play on the American distrust of foreigners, although it should be noted that in her fourth novel, *Clarence*, the villainous Henriques Pedrillo is revealed to be an American in disguise. But in *A New-England Tale*, the foreigner is exposed and tarred and feathered, and Elvira is left with her shame.

Mrs. Wilson's son David, the second example of those "denied the appropriate pleasures of youth," is "driven to sins of a much deeper die than those which Mrs. Wilson sought to avoid."[25] David, we learn, is "a headstrong youth of seventeen," whose passions have been "curbed by the authority of his mother, but never tamed."[26] Among other evils, David has seduced sweet young Mary Oakley. With her baby by David, Mary arrives at his home only to have him turn her away; and both she and the child die in the cottage of the woodsman who found them in the forest.

Not content with statutory rape, David next steals five hundred dollars from his mother, for which crime "bless'd" Jane is, naturally, accused. David now moves to mail robbery but is captured. The punishment for his crime is death, but he escapes from prison; and the last we hear of him, he is planning to flee to the West Indies. Before sailing, however, he sends a note to his mother in which he blames her—in some respects unjustly—for being the cause of the life he has led. "Mother, mother! oh, that I must call you so!" he raves, "—as I do it, I howl a curse with every breath—you have destroyed me."[27] In a sense, the son's denunciation is poetic justice, in Sedgwick terms; for his mother once said of her recently deceased daughter "I have no reason to hope for her. She died without repentance."[28]

The third—and also the flimsiest—of Miss Sedgwick's young villains is Edward Erskine. He seems little more than a vehicle for sermons about corrupt law practices, gambling, and dueling. Unfortunately, A *New-England Tale* did not end the sermonizing instinct in Miss Sedgwick, for all three themes reappeared in *Clarence*. Against the four villains—Mrs. Wilson, Elvira, David, and Edward Erskine—Miss Sedgwick places her ideal: Jane Elton, whose somewhat colorless character is Miss Sedgwick's illustration of an ideal Christian woman. Jane's character is colorless precisely because she never acts decisively and meekly endures the false accusations of her enemies. It is clear that no Jane Elton will ever rid the world of evil; Jane simply maintains her Christian outlook on life, never despairs, nurses the sick, and helps the downtrodden. In other words, she is the embodiment of faith, hope, and charity. It is left for men such as Mr. Lloyd to combat actively the evil in the world and to insure a "happy ending" for women like Jane. In this case, the "happy ending" occurs when Jane is united in connubial bliss to the holy Quaker and returns to the love and tender kindness of Mary Hull, the faithful domestic.

It may be worth adding here that, throughout Miss Sedgwick's writings, marriage is shown to provide the best and happiest life for women. Just as Miss Sedgwick's first novel ends with a marriage, so does her last, *Married or Single?*, which demonstrates that, while a woman may live a productive and happy life as a single woman, she may find herself even more useful and happy if she is married to a good man. Although Miss Sedgwick remained single, she never ceased to believe that, if a woman found the right man, her life would be ideally happy. All Miss Sedgwick's heroines are rewarded with marriage—generally at the very end of the novel.

Even if A *New-England Tale* had been concerned solely with corrupt law practices, gambling, and dueling, it might have been a sensation in its day. The novel portrayed a minister—the man who gave Mrs. Elton's funeral sermon —in an unfavorable way; and it also showed Mrs. Wilson, a pillar of the local church and a strict Calvinist, to be uncharitable and cruel. Furthermore, the hero of the novel was a Quaker, one whose religion had its origins in Pennsylvania, not New England. Surely there were some read-

ers of the novel who knew that the original Calvinist settlers of New England had tortured and hanged Quakers
who were thought to be dangerous and pernicious heretics
who might corrupt the minds of the young. Because the
novel portrayed Calvinism in an unfavorable light, Congre-
gationalists, Presbyterians, and other Calvinists were out-
raged. A viper—and that viper a socially élite Sedgwick!—
had emerged from within. Predictably, the book became
something of a sensation in New England, and Miss Sedgwick's brother was soon able to write to her that the publishers had "increased orders from the booksellers."[29]

IV *The Yankee*

One aspect of *A New-England Tale* which continued to
interest readers long after its religious attitudes ceased
to be controversial was Miss Sedgwick's use of New England
manners and dialect; Cooper referred to this aspect of the
novel when he wrote that of the "books which profess to
illustrate American society and manners, we have never
met with one which so perfectly and agreeably accom-
lishes the design, to a certain extent, as" *A New-England
Tale.*[30]

The scene of the book was obviously Stockbridge and
the surrounding countryside, including one crossroads
village, the town of Becket, Massachusetts, which Miss
Sedgwick cited by name in the novel. Becket is given
as the home of a storekeeper—he specializes in cake
and beer—and his wife Tempy, short for Temperance; his
children, Desdemony, Valorous, Octavy, Rodolphus, and
Soloman Wheeler. Miss Sedgwick's storekeeper is the first
in American fiction to represent the Yankee peddler or
"dealer in notions," one of the stock figures in American
myth.[31]

Later developments of this figure such as Seba Smith's
Jack Downing (1830) portrayed him as a loner and as a man
who brought the amenities of civilization—clocks, hats,
knives, and so forth—to the frontier, where he sold
them at an enormous profit. In addition to being a good
salesman, the Yankee peddler also demonstrated a fine
wit; and this characteristic is most evident in Miss Sedg-

wick's storekeeper. Furthermore, Miss Sedgwick carefully
recorded the storekeeper's pronunciation—or rather mis-
pronunciation—of English. She was not the first writer
to use the New England dialect in literature—Royall
Tyler's *The Contrast* (1787) is among the earlier works
in which this particular dialect is found—but *A New-
England Tale* was one of the first works of prose fiction
to use colloquial Yankee language.

New England dialect was used extensively in short
stories and novels by later writers, notably Harriet Beecher
Stowe and Sarah Orne Jewett; but Miss Sedgwick used
it seldom. Her only other novel which uses it at length
is *Redwood,* where a character named Deborah Lenox
always speaks in colloquial Yankee language. Clearly
Miss Sedgwick did not find New England dialect as interesting as, for example, Sarah Orne Jewett did—Miss
Jewett in *The Country of the Pointed Firs* created a town
in which virtually everyone speaks colloquially—but, as the
following passage from *A New-England Tale* indicates,
Miss Sedgwick could use this kind of language effectively
and humorously when she wished. "Why friend," says
the Becket storekeeper during a storm,

you look scare't, pretty pokerish weather, to be sure, but then
we don't mind it up here. . . . But last week, . . . there was
the most *tedious* spell of weather I have seen sen the week before
last thanksgiving [sic], when my wife and I went down into
the lower part of Becket, to hear Deacon Hollister's funeral
sarmont—Don't you remember, Tempy, that musical fellow
that was there?—"I don't see," says he, "the use of the minister
preaching up so much about hell-fire," says he, "it is a very
good doctrine," says he, "to preach down on Connecticut River,
but," says he, "I should not think it would frighten any body
in such a cold place as Becket."[32]

In the speech of the Becket storekeeper, we see the
beginnings of a tradition of folk humor in fiction that con-
tinued through Seba Smith, Thomas Haliburton, Josh
Billings—born in the nearby town of Lanesborough—and
Artemus Ward until it reached the Mississippi and Mark
Twain fifty years later.

But if *A New-England Tale* still has interest because of

its use of New England characters and language, it also
is read because of one of its characters, "Crazy Bet." She
is, as Miss Sedgwick notes in her Preface, the only figure
in the book directly based on an actual person. The original was Miss Susan Dunham, who for fifty years made a
destinationless pilgrimage of mourning throughout the
towns of Berkshire County. "Crazy Sue," as she was called,
was born on Martha's Vineyard; but at an early age she
moved to Savoy, a small Berkshire hill town, where she
fell in love with one whose father stood politically at
opposite poles from her own. The couple was, therefore,
forbidden to marry. Some time afterwards, she went to a
religious gathering; "got the spirit"; and, romantically
combining grief over lost love with an intense faith,
promptly went insane.

She began soon after her lifelong pilgrimage. Whenever
there was sickness in a village, Sue would arrive, dressed
in mourning. "Any happening of a tragic nature," notes
her biographer, "speedily brought her to the scene of the
event," where "she would hover in and about . . . until
the people had quieted down."[33] She also derived some satisfaction from visiting graveyards, particularly at night,
where "she would sing and pray and sometimes utter
loud moanings, and so wildly shriek that aroused sleepers
would tremble for fear that some horrid crime was being
enacted."[34] In Lanesborough, there was a door knocker
attached to the winter tomb; and, when Sue visited the
town, she often made a midnight visit to the tomb, where
she banged the knocker and attempted to wake the dead.
Many homes in the county welcomed her whenever she
passed through; and one of them, it should not be surprising to learn, was the home of Theodore Sedgwick.[35]

The "Crazy Bet" of *A New-England Tale* is substan-
tially the same as this historical figure of Susan Dunham
—a frequenter of camp meetings, a mourner at funerals,
and an inhabitant of graveyards. She has, however, no-
ticeably little relevance to the novel in proportion to her
interest for the reader. That such a minor character should
in the end assume so much importance, should be the most
fully, or at least the most interestingly, developed person

in the book, suggests how poorly the author understood at this point the nature of fiction.

V *The New American Literature*

A *New-England Tale* is primarily remembered for its historical importance. It appeared about the same time as Irving's *The Sketch Book,* Cooper's *The Spy* and *The Pioneers,* and Bryant's early poems; and the fact that it was so highly praised in its own day—by Cooper, among others—may be explained, at least in part, by the attempt then being made to discover a truly American literature. As for other favorable reviewers, Miss Edgeworth might have been more critical had the book not been dedicated to her; and, when one English reviewer stated that "this little tale is on the whole a favorable specimen of American talent and feeling," it was not necessary to look far to discover how low the British estimation of "American talent and feeling" was.[36]

Of those who criticized the book most severely, the moral and theological critics were answered in the preface to the second edition: "the objections which have been made to the moral and religious character of this book, the writer cannot comprehend. . . . Religious cant and sanctimonious pretense have existed in most ages of the world, and have ever been deemed legitimate objects of satire."[37] In the same preface, Miss Sedgwick added, with circumlocution, that, "if the writer could suppose that any reader of intelligence and candour could consider this tale as a designed attack upon the character of any class of christians [sic], such an object would be distinctly disavowed."[38] Calvinists, it seems, are not Christians. Disfavor with the book on religious grounds continued; for, as late as 1852, the time of a new edition, one critic wrote that "we must acknowledge that it is a more perilous undertaking to ridicule religious excesses,—and . . . we must in candor say that we think Miss Sedgwick has erred upon the more dangerous side."[39]

The other aspect of the book that attracted attention— Miss Sedgwick's use of local color—was a promising sign, for her critics always welcomed her use of American and particularly New England settings and characters. Although few of her novels use dialect, many of them do make use of specifically New England settings as well as New England characters such as the Lenoxes, the Yankee farmers in *Redwood*. In *A New-England Tale*, there are brief descriptions of Berkshire scenery as well as such decidedly New England characters as the Becket storekeeper. Furthermore, the intolerant Calvinists the novel attacks were largely found in New England. However, there is nothing which distinguishes the heroine Jane Elton as a Yankee.

Until Miss Sedgwick wrote her didactic tale *Home* in 1835, she avoided characterizing her heroes and heroines as New Englanders. Instead, her ideal figures are characterized largely by faith, hope, and charity—Christian virtues which Miss Sedgwick is careful not to associate with any one section of the country but which she implies may be found everywhere. She did associate domesticity with New England or felt at least that domestic life had its major advocates in New England families; and so in *Home*, she made her central characters explicitly New Englanders, always longing to return to their family home in the Berkshire hills. However, in her earlier works, including *A New-England Tale*, local color was generally relegated to the characterization of minor figures and to the description of scenery.

There are a very large number of serious flaws in the book, and the most serious involves the superficial characterization of Jane Elton. Furthermore, Mr. Lloyd is virtually uncharacterized. Miss Sedgwick tells her readers that he is a good man and a Quaker and that he has considerable interest in Jane's welfare, but little is done to characterize him beyond this point. There are other problems of this sort: Mrs. Wilson's sisters, for example, are rather lifeless villains. Neither of these sisters is willing to admit that there is any good in Jane, and neither is willing to adopt her, but little more is said about them. Although the ostensible purpose of the novel is to attack religious hypocrisy and intolerance, the most interesting character in the book, "Crazy Bet," attracts the reader's attention because of her eccentricities rather than because she recognizes Jane's moral characteristics.

Finally, it should be noted that the novel's Cinderella ending in which Jane marries Mr. Lloyd is not entirely satisfactory. Although novels during this period often ended with at least one marriage (Cooper's *The Pioneers* (1823), for example ends with the marriage of his virtuous heroine), Jane is such a thoroughly passive woman, incapable of defending herself against even the most blatantly false accusations, that her marriage to Mr. Lloyd seems altogether too fortuitous—something which would happen to few women as withdrawn, passive, and self-effacing as she. Indeed, Miss Sedgwick makes it clear that, if Mr. Lloyd had not learned of Jane's plight from one of his servants, he never would have come to her rescue.

But whatever weaknesses the book possesses—and Miss Sedgwick herself held it in very low esteem—there is no question how the Sedgwick brothers felt.[40] "I have read 130 pages of the book," wrote Theodore. "It exceeds all my expectations, fond and flattering as they were."[41] And Henry added that "I think, dear Kate, that your destiny is now fixed. . . . I don't know of any thing which now gives me so much excitement as the certain prospect of your future eminence."[42]

CHAPTER *3*

Down on the Farm;
or, *Redwood* Revisited

[Miss Sedgwick] has chosen ground hitherto unoccupied, as
the scene of her narrative; and while the moral of her story . . .
is obviously her chief aim, her materials are purely domestic;
and in the delineation of her characters, and the incidents into
which the personages she describes are thrown, we recognize
what we have all seen and heard and observed, but what no one
yet has so faithfully depicted.
                    — *The Atlantic Magazine*, review of *Redwood*.[1]

MISS Sedgwick's second novel, *Redwood* (1824), "is in
such high esteem," Bryant wrote to her brother
Charles, "that it is absolutely dangerous and unsafe not
to admire it . . . and what is better still [is] that those who
for some reason or other (probably religious prejudices)
did not like the *New England Tale* have come out its decided and redoubtable champions."[2] *Redwood* was favorably compared with the novels of Cooper and Sir Walter
Scott; and, since the book was published anonymously,
there was considerable debate as to the identity of the
author; and many concluded that it must be Cooper himself. There were, to be sure, those who attacked the novel;
but they were the minority. *Redwood* proved to be with
both critics and the public one of the most successful novels of
of its day—on both sides of the Atlantic.

But while *Redwood* is a good novel, far superior to
A New-England Tale, it is structurally far from perfect.
Its faults, however, are common with other fiction of
the era. Too often its approach, which seems to foreshadow
the realistic novels of the latter part of the century, slides
off unaccountably into sentimentality and ineffective

melodrama. It is not very likely that modern readers will be moved, as Miss Sedgwick's contemporaries were, by Peggy, the poor blind girl, and by "Billy Raymond, the lame boy that supported his old mother by fishing."[3] The novel also relies too often on timeworn plot conventions. The carriage accident with which the book opens and on which the meeting of Henry Redwood and Ellen Bruce depends is, as Cowie has pointed out, "a device used with shameless frequency by novelists of the time."[4] More important is the author's unavailing attempt to rework the hidden-identity theme, which, as Bryant noted, is one of *Redwood's* major defects.[5] Ellen's hidden identity and various other plot conventions lead the author at times into producing a novel that had already been written many times before.

The virtues of *Redwood* are not in its telling but in its overall concept of a world that is not controlled by romantic fancy but by convention, habit, and circumstance. *Redwood* is historically important, therefore, as one of the first examples of the Realistic novel in America.

I *Plot and Subplots*

Redwood opens in Vermont, where aristocratic Southerner Henry Redwood and his daughter Caroline have been traveling. He is injured in a carriage accident and is invited by the Lenoxes, a farming family, to stay at their home while he recuperates. Redwood is glad to accept the invitation; but Caroline considers the Lenoxes to be her social inferiors and would prefer to travel to the city or to a summer resort. Caroline is especially distressed to find herself unfavorably compared with another guest at the Lenox home, Ellen Bruce. Ellen is virtuous and kind; she is "disinterested," concerned only with the welfare of others, not her own well-being. On the other hand, Caroline is selfish, conceited, and haughty. While her father is recuperating, Charles Westall, a Southerner whom her father hopes she will marry, visits the Redwoods at the Lenox family. He is attracted to Ellen; and it is she, not Caroline, whom he decides to marry.

When the setting of the novel shifts to Lebanon, New York, a summer resort near Massachusetts, Ellen proves herself as socially agreeable as she is virtuous. The novel ends with marriages of Ellen to Charles and of Caroline to a fortune hunter. Before this happens, however, the discovery is made that Ellen is really Redwood's daughter from a youthful marriage to a servant—a marriage of which his father disapproved in the belief that no servant girl was worthy of marriage into the aristocratic Redwood family. Unknown to Redwood, his wife, who had died shortly after he left to travel abroad, gave birth to a daughter, Ellen, who has been reared by friends in New England. Meanwhile, Redwood has married a second time, and the child of this marriage is Caroline. Ellen is not told who her father is until her twenty-first birthday, which occurs shortly after Mr. Redwood's arrival at the Lenox farm, where coincidence brings father and daughter together for the first time.

Redwood's subplot involves Susan and Emily Allen, relatives of the Lenox family. Emily has been convinced by Susan, her aunt, to join a Hancock, Massachusetts, Shaker community—a Christian community in which the members take a vow of chastity. However, when one of the men, Reuben Harrington, is attracted to Emily, he abducts her from the community and tries to seduce her. At the end of the episode, she is rescued by friends and members of her family. Of the other characters of significance, the most important is Aunt Deborah Lenox, the sister of the farmer at whose house Redwood stays while he is recuperating. Because she comments frequently about Ellen's virtues and Caroline's vices, she serves as Miss Sedgwick's moral commentator in the story. Furthermore, in the second half of the novel, the girl Grace Campbell is introduced. She comes from the aristocracy of Pennsylvania; and, like Caroline, she has grown up in a wealthy family and has enjoyed the advantages of education and travel. However, unlike Caroline, she has become as virtuous as Ellen. As Miss Sedgwick's virtuous aristocrat, she contrasts to Caroline, the aristocrat who offers the world little except vanity and wealth.

Redwood's plot clearly suggests that Miss Sedgwick believed that the "good" seldom receive their rewards in this world. Although the novel ends with Ellen's marriage to Charles Westall, the wealthy Southerner, this occasion is one of the few in which virtue is materially rewarded. For more than twenty-one years, Ellen has been deprived of the advantages of education, travel, and good society which her father's money and social position could have offered her but which have been lavished on Caroline. Charles, an idealist, states that "the decision of natural justice" is "that the fault of one person cannot be transferred to another—that it cannot be right to make an innocent child suffer for the guilt of its parent."[6] However, "natural justice" and the moral dictums of Charles Westall do not govern the story; and, if all turns out "right" in the end, it is, nonetheless, true that the innocent, not the guilty, have suffered first.

Miss Sedgwick spares no words in telling her readers— primarily through the comments of Charles Westall and Deborah Lenox—what the world *should* be like; but her own moral beliefs do not prevent her from showing the world as it is. As Harriet Martineau wrote, Miss Sedgwick, the American counterpart of Jane Austen, created "fiction which is, as nearly as possible, a transcript of actual life."[7] Although there would later be closer transcripts of "actual life," *Redwood* was an exception to the tradition of the Romance with which American fiction was almost entirely associated in the early years of its development.

II *The Central Characters*

Caroline Redwood is a more interesting character than Ellen Bruce. Caroline's mother, we learn, was the vain Maria Manning; and she had been reared by her grandmother who had lavished on her "a twofold measure of the indulgencies and flatteries that had spoiled the mother."[8] At the opening of the novel, Caroline is eighteen, "the idol of the fashionable world, and as completely *au fait* in all its arts and mysteries, as a veteran belle of five and twenty."[9] Taught by her grandmother—whom

Miss Sedgwick perhaps patterned along the lines of one of her ancestors—"that people of fortune should never lay aside the insignia of their rank," Caroline has decided that the only things in life which hold an interest for her are "the drawing-room, the ball-room, and the other haunts of the beau monde."[10] As to her male companions, they must be "accomplished," meaning "does he speak french [sic]? does he dance well? Is he genteel and elegant, and all that?"[11] Caroline tells her grandmother that the town in which the Lenoxes live is a "vile place," and the Lenoxes themselves "are common working vulgar farmers."[12] "They toil on," she notes with astonishment, "as if it was a pleasure."[13] And later she tells a friend, "I found it quite impossible to make those people feel they were not my equals."[14] While attending a funeral at the Vermont farmhouse, Caroline watches the mourners "with the indifference with which she would have regarded the shifting scenes of a wearisome play."[15] Asked if she wishes to see the corpse, she replies, "I have no fancy for looking at dead people, and certainly I shall not look at one dead that I never saw living."[16]

If we enjoy this particular kind of sarcasm, Caroline can be a very entertaining character; but, of course, she has a more important place in the novel than that of a comic figure. Caroline's pride interests the author since it is a pride which prevents her from participating sympathetically in the lives of those around her, and which makes her the primary contrast with Ellen.

Ellen's grandfather was disowned by his father for the "unpardonable" sin of marrying "beneath his station," and her mother was considered to be very much her father's inferior socially.[17] In short, Ellen's ancestry is somewhat less distinguished that Caroline's. However, Ellen has received "lessons in practical life" from her adopted family in New England; and a neighbor has provided her with "taste and skill in drawing, . . knowledge of french and italian [sic], and all those arts of female handicraft . . . of her day." Likewise, she has learned "to explore the records of history, and to delight in the bright creations of poetry."[18] Although Ellen apparently has no practical use for her rather substantial learning, it is clear that her education, though different, is no less significant than Caroline Redwood's. (It is worth noting that American literary heroines of the nineteenth century were customarily provided with an education at least as extensive as Ellen's, but their prodigious learning was seldom, if ever, put to any use.)

While Caroline is vain and self-centered, Ellen is frequently said to be "disinterested," a characteristic which is common to all Miss Sedgwick's heroes and heroines. "Ellen [is] at that age when sentiment controls interest"; she is an "enthusiast" as indeed are many of Miss Sedgwick's favorites, including Grace Herbert in *Married or Single?* and Hope Leslie in the novel of that name.[19] Ellen, however, is one of the author's least colorful heroines— although she represents a definite improvement over Jane Elton. *Redwood* does not provide Ellen with sufficiently major opportunities to prove that she is really the ideal woman—the "disinterested" and virtuous enthusiast— which her associates claim she is. "There is something singularly pure and lovely in her whole expression and manner, in perfect unison with her disinterested conduct" says Charles Westall.[20] Fittingly, it is he—likewise described as "disinterested"—who marries Ellen; for selfish Caroline is left to the mercies of a fortune hunter.[21]

Ellen and Caroline's father, Henry Redwood, son of a wealthy planter, has fallen under the influence of two men, Edmund Westall, Charles' father, who has the positive, Christian influence, and Mr. Alsop, who is as thoroughly evil as David and Elvira Wilson in *A New-England Tale.* The result is that Redwood's "destiny through life [is] to feel right and to act wrong."[22] This conflict within him is dramatized externally in the moral conflict between Caroline and Ellen, and their conflict is elaborated through contrasts with the minor figures. These characters include the other Redwoods and Westalls from the South, the Campbells and Armsteads from Pennsylvania, and the Allens and Lenoxes from New England. In the second group, the families from Pennsylvania, the only figure of any great importance is Grace Campbell; and she combines the virtues of Ellen with the colorfulness of Caroline and thereby acts as a ballast to the somewhat dry and somber heroine. Miss Sedgwick's placing her heroes and villains in the South, New England, and Pennsylvania, is important because this distribution represents an attempt, even if a crude one, to make her novel a truly American one.

The Lenoxes may have been patterned after any one of a number of undistinguished families with which Miss Sedgwick was acquainted—ones that, however, produced eminent sons. Mr. Lenox, we are told, "belonged to the mass of New-England farmers, was industrious and frugal, sober and temperate, and enjoyed the reward of these staple virtues, good health and a competency."[23] "His wife (we believe not a singular case in matrimonial history)," says Miss Sedgwick "was his superior: intelligent, well-informed, enterprising, and efficient."[24] One of their sons is educated at Harvard and becomes a minister, and another goes west to Ohio to found a settlement. At home are two sons and four girls "diligent, good-humoured, and intelligent."[25] "There is nothing in New-England so eagerly sought for, or so highly prized by all classes of people," wrote Miss Sedgwick in her first novel, "as the advantages of education."[26] Consequently, the Lenox children hike a mile and a half to hear a lecture on botany, something that Caroline, unlike Ellen, would never think of doing.

The most important member of this Vermont family is Deborah Lenox, the embodiment of a Yankee common sense that is somewhat colored, however, by sentimentality. What she has to say can generally be taken, as we have observed, as the author's own comments. Deborah, who is Mr. Lenox's sister, "looks upon herself as a natural protector of the weak and oppressed."[27] Once in love with "a veteran soldier, who . . . was captivated by the martial air of this then young Amazon," she now has only one thing left as a sign of her romance, a string of gold beads he once gave her, her "only relict of worldly or womanly vanity."[28] The practical-minded Deborah, we read, "would not voluntarily encumber herself with any toilette duties that could in decency be dispensed with." She never put "any covering on her hair, which time had now considerably grisled; but she wore it confined in one long braid, and so closely bound with a black ribbon, that it did not require, in her judgment, more than a weekly adjustment."[29]

Deborah, as might be expected, has little affection for the girl she calls "that *Caroliny gal,* with all her flaunting ruffles and folderols."[30] Miss Redwood in turn spares no love for Deborah; she considers her a "demi-savage," and an "oddity . . , whom they call an 'old girl;' a hideous monster—a giantess; I suspect a descendant of the New England witches."[31] Caroline is plainly offended to see anyone, even her father, receiving the attention that she considers rightfully hers. "I hear [Deborah] at this moment," she writes her grandmother, "bawling to one of the boys, to kill the black-eared pig,—for [my father] no doubt. Notwithstanding her devotion to papa, she does not pay me the least respect."[32] While Ellen seldom thinks of herself and spends her time helping those who need her, Caroline is conceited and vain. She is concerned with the welfare of no one but herself, and this fact is emphasized in Deborah's comments.

III   *Shakers and Seduction*

Redwood's subplot, as has been stated, involves the Shaker community or, as they called themselves, "The Millenial Church" and "The United Society of Believers in Christ's Second Coming." Their curious form of religious service is described by Miss Sedgwick:

After a few moments, the deep and reverential silence of the assembly was broken by a shout, in which every voice was simultaneously lifted to its highest pitch. The shout was followed by a hymn, but sung so loud, with such discordant and irregular sounds, (for music it could not be called) that it was impossible to distinguish any words, excepting "our mother" and "mother Anne," [*sic*] which seemed to form a kind of chorus. The singing was accompanied by an equal and steady motion, an alternating from one foot to the other, which resembles to a profane eye the *bas pas* of the world's dancers. The deafening yell and uniform motion continued till their breath was spent, when all the assembly, as if governed by one instinct, lapsed into silence.[33]

In 1824, when *Redwood* was published, the Shakers were rapidly becoming one of the larger religious organizations in the United States. In 1776, Ann Lee, who claimed that she was the female counterpart of Christ, founded the first American Shaker community in Watervliet, New York. Variously styling herself as "Mother Ann" and as "Ann the Word," she soon had enough converts to establish further communities. The movement continued to spread until Shaker settlements existed throughout much of the country.

Some New Englanders undoubtedly felt that the Shakers posed a threat to traditional patterns of life in the Northeast. Through the Shakers' social practices—they never married, and they held all property in common—they were quite consciously undermining the established institutions of church, town, and family, all of which were revered in New England. The Shakers believed intensely in their own ways of life, and they were able to convince the sons and daughters of many New England families to become Shakers. According to members of "The Millenial Church," only in their communities was life truly Christian, only there could the New Jerusalem be found— a belief which was surely not welcomed by New Englanders who remembered that their Puritan ancestors had come to the New World to found their own Jerusalem, one free from the doctrines of all other religious groups.

Miss Sedgwick admired the Shakers' "practical wisdom," but she was unwilling to grant that they were as Godly as they claimed to be.[34] She cited, for example, the fact that the society was ruled by " 'elder brothers' and 'elder sisters,' "—and then she vindictively noted—"whose 'gifts' of superior wisdom, knowledge, or cunning, obtain for them these titles, and secure to them their rights and immunities."[35] Miss Sedgwick, like her fellow New Englanders, believed that the Shaker communities were not the paradises that their members said they were but rather were deeply flawed. She believed that "Mother Ann" was "by the charitable deemed an enthusiast—by those of a severer judgment, an imposter"; and, while Miss Sedgwick was not willing to call "the Word" "an imposter," neither was she willing to call her a pure "enthusiast" in the sense that the term is used to describe Ellen Bruce and Charles Westall.[36] For all her "practical wisdom," Mother Ann, concluded Miss Sedgwick, was possessed by "the wildest fanaticism."[37]

Miss Sedgwick, furthermore, could not accept the Shakers' assertion that sin grew from what they labelled "natural affections." Satan "has taken advantage of her late visit to her kindred" one Shaker remarks of Emily Allen, "and has carried her back to the path of natural affection, out of which she had travelled far—and seeing nature reviving, and grace sleeping, he hath taken that moment to bind her again with carnal bonds."[38] But, as Miss Sedgwick makes clear, whatever the accused Emily has been victimized by, it has been neither the devil nor natural affections.

Emily, who is memorably described as "the simple amiable little fanatic," is a member of the Shaker community in Hancock, Massachusetts.[39] She is abducted by Reuben Harrington, a Shaker who is considered by his brethren to be one of their most virtuous members but who is characterized by another as the "master-devil."[40] Emily is rescued by her friends, and Harrington, who has ironically said of others that "they must drink the bitter draught their own folly has mixed," is captured but is then released "to wander upon the earth, despised and avoided, enduring all the misery of . . . unrepented guilt."[41] Emily has clearly been the victim, not the disciple, of sin; it was not her response to her "natural affections" that injured her. On the other hand, it is clear that Harrington might never have caused the trouble he did—or even have become a respected elder—if the other members of the Shaker community had noted his lack of charity, kindness, and forgiveness—in short, his lack of natural affections. Harrington claims that sin proceeds "from the heart."[42] However, Miss Sedgwick insists that the Shakers, by ignoring their natural affections (the heart), avoid virtue as well.

The Shakers' emotional life is cold and is isolated from the rest of the world. Their desire to avoid natural affection is reflected in a number of passages and descriptions—"their austere formality," their "uniform habits and monotonous occupations," which "have a strong tendency to check every irregular feeling, and to intercept every vagrant desire," and, finally, their ability to "condemn the delight that springs from natural beauty."[43] The Shakers, no New Jerusalem, are left by Miss Sedgwick on "the frozen summits where they remained secure, regarding with equal contempt the earthly influences that bless and fertilize, or ravage and destroy."[44]

IV *The Enemy*

Deborah Lenox, describing Ellen's moral strength, exclaims that " 'it is not being born here or there, it is not habit; it is not strength of limb, but here,' [striking] her hand against her heart, 'here is what gives Ellen Bruce strength and patience.' "[45] But, while the heart, the "natural affections," are of great importance, the world is not always controlled by them. Vanity as well as charity can mold character. Caroline has grown up in an aristocratic Southern family which has taught her to regard herself as a better person than most other people in the world. Her family's vanity is based solely on wealth and standing in Southern society. Caroline's background has made her what she is: a vain, frivolous, and selfish woman.

On the other hand, Ellen, who has been exposed to a simpler life in a New England family in which no one has either enough money or ancestors to claim membership in aristocracy, has been reared in an environment in which most people devote their time to performing Christian acts of charity. Indeed, Mr. and Mrs. Allen have reared her, even though she is not their daughter, because they consider doing so their Christian duty. Consequently, both Caroline and Ellen may be viewed as products of their respective environments. Charles Westall, who has much to say about the way in which the world should be run, feels that no one should unjustly suffer.[46] However, the world in *Redwood* does not conduct itself according to Charles' sense of justice. According to this novel, people are born innocent and then molded "by the earthly influences that bless and fertilize, or ravage and destroy."[47]

The emphasis on convention, habit, and circumstance is backed by a heavy use of Realistic detail, particularly in the use of characteristics of New England personalities and settings. Deborah Lenox speaks New England dialect; and the members of the Lenox family, as previously noted, are characterized by Miss Sedgwick as decidedly New England types—the hard-working and parsimonious father, his more intelligent and enterprising wife, and his children eager to acquire all the education available to them. Caroline's desire for a life of social diversions is counterpointed by the New Englanders' willingness to hike a mile and half to hear a lecture on botany.

Miss Sedgwick sets her novel not only at Eton, Vermont, but also at Hancock, Massachusetts, and the Shaker settlement located there. In describing the religious services of the Shaker settlement at Hancock, Miss Sedgwick was dealing with the practices of a religious sect which was especially strong in the Northeast, although, in fact, communities of Shakers were found throughout the country. Finally, in a few chapters toward the end of *Redwood,* Miss Sedgwick placed the action in Lebanon, New York, a summer resort or watering place not far from the Shaker community at Hancock. In 1824 when the novel was published, Lebanon was second only to Saratoga Springs, New York, among the fashionable watering places in the country. Here, among the wealthiest and most cultivated of the nation's aristocrats, Ellen proves herself to be as well mannered and polite as the best educated and socially cultivated women at the resort. Clearly Miss Sedgwick did not choose her settings capriciously; the settings—Vermont, the Shaker community in Massachusetts, and Lebanon—are employed in the definition of character and in the movement of the plot.

"It is the peculiar province of [the novel]," wrote Miss Sedgwick in her preface to *Redwood,* "to denote the passing character and manners of the present time and place." [48] Her primary objectives included "the delinia

tion of American life and character," a field in which,
said one mid-century critic, she and Cooper "can be considered pioneers."[49] Although she described characters
from places other than New England—the Redwoods were,
for example, from Virginia and South Carolina—most
of her fiction is set in the Northeast and most of her heroes
and many of her villains are Yankees. Not all New England
received Miss Sedgwick's approval, of course; as A New-
England Tale makes clear, she had little sympathy with
uncharitable Calvinists, and in Redwood, she condemned
the Shakers for their lack of trust in "natural affections."
Miss Sedgwick's ideal New Englanders are people like
Deborah Lenox and the other members of her family who
freely express their "natural affections" and try to find
goodness, not original sin, in other people. However,
Miss Sedgwick emphasized that ideal people like Deborah
Lenox were surely not to be found only in New England; and
she offered in Redwood the example of the Southern
gentleman Charles Westall who perceives Ellen's goodness
as fully as Deborah Lenox does.

V Sedgwick and Cooper

As stated above, Redwood was enthusiastically received
on both sides of the Atlantic. The book was reprinted
in England and translated into Spanish, Italian, Swedish,
German, and French. Writing from England, Maria
Edgeworth stated that the novel appeared to her to be

a work of superior talent, far greater than even 'The New-England Tale' gave me reason to expect. The character of Aunt
Deborah is first rate—in Scott's best manner, yet not an imitation
of Scott. It is to America what Scott's characters are to Scotland,
valuable as original pictures, with enough of individual pe-
culiarity to be interesting, and to give the feeling of reality
and life as portraits, with sufficient also of general characteristics to give them the philosophical merit of portraying a class.[50]

In America, William Cullen Bryant was especially
enthusiastic about her use of regional characteristics
and settings. He told   readers of The North American

Review that Miss Sedgwick "has come down to the very days in which we live, to quiet times and familiar manners, and has laid the scene of her narrative in the most ancient and tranquil parts of our country; presenting us not merely with the picture of what she has imagined, but with the copy of what she has observed."[51] When he wrote this statement, Bryant was a very close friend of the Sedgwick family; indeed the book was dedicated to him. Nonetheless, he reviewed the book objectively, criticizing it heavily for its use of the hidden-identity device; however, the conclusion of his review was favorable. "We look upon [*Redwood*]," he wrote, "as a conclusive argument, that the writers of fiction of which the scene is laid in familiar and domestic life, have a rich and varied field before them in the United States."[52]

"Redwood [*sic*] sells very well," Miss Sedgwick's brother Henry wrote to her. "The sale is constantly increasing, and the booksellers say it is now better than [Sir Walter Scott's] Redgauntlet [*sic*]."[53] And he was able to report two months later that "the booksellers are all teasing me to know when another work will come from the author of 'Redwood.' They say it will go as well or better than one from Cooper or Irving."[54] *Redwood*, the critic John S. Hart wrote several years later, "was received at once with a degree of favour that caused the author's name to be associated, and on equal terms, with that of Cooper, who was then at the height of his popularity."[55] Indeed, in France the critics decided that *Redwood* must be his work. In both Italy and France, *Redwood* was published with Cooper's name on the title page.[56] "Harry was told last evening," wrote Miss Sedgwick, "that there was a dispute in the Paris newspapers whether [*Redwood*] was or was not written by Cooper. It is to be hoped that Mr. C.'s self-complacency will not be wounded by this mortifying news."[57]

VI *The Other Sedgwicks*

One book on which *Redwood* seems to have had an immediate effect was *Hints to My Countrymen* (1826), a semi-fictional work by Miss Sedgwick's brother Theodore. Unfortunately, Theodore's book, while interesting, was primarily a somewhat shallow battle cry for the common man. Although *The North American Review* gave the book a fairly generous notice, the magazine stated that it would have been of far greater value had it been more critical of what it praised.[58] Nonetheless, *Hints to My Countrymen* added to the figures of the Yankee which the author's sister had been developing. We find, for example, the following description, based in part perhaps on one of Miss Sedgwick's ancestors. "I do not recollect your great-grandfather," one of the characters tells another, "but they have often described him to me. He resided about the year 1756, at Hatfield, in Massachusetts. That country was then much disturbed by the Indians. He used to go to church with a lead-headed cane in his hands, a gun on his shoulder, and with a bullet pouch in front: being a proud man, they used to say his gun was of no use; for that he carried his head so high, that he could never see an Indian in the bushes."[59]

Meanwhile, another of Miss Sedgwick's brothers, Henry Dwight, had written in *The North American Review* that "in this country, and in that from which we derive our legal institutions, the law is *artificial and technical* to an extent very much beyond what is required by the reason or nature of the case."[60] Henry Dwight Sedgwick's desire to reform the common law eventually had a positive result in the work of his disciple David Dudley Field, Jr., whose legal reforms were of international and national significance. Henry Dwight and Robert Sedgwick also made known their sympathy with the Greek cause in the Greek War of Independence. Their sympathies and their legal efforts on behalf of the Greek cause involved them in a furious pamphlet war that occupied the public mind for many years.

During the 1820's, Theodore, Henry Dwight, Robert, and Catharine Sedgwick became prominent and important figures in their respective professions. Her brothers' public successes, as well as their personal interest in her writings, encouraged Miss Sedgwick to pursue her work as a writer; but she never considered her writing to be more important than her family: she was always willing to neglect her work when there was an opportunity for a reunion with her brothers and sisters.

Between the publications of her major novels, *Redwood* (1824) and *Hope Leslie* (1827), Miss Sedgwick published *The Travellers* (1825) and *The Deformed Boy* (1826), both books for children. The first, a travel narrative concerning a journey to Montreal by way of Western New York State, has no literary pretensions. *The Deformed Boy,* an instructional narrative, teaches children the need for human sympathy and understanding. The deformed boy of the title has a poor, sick mother who is unable to care for either herself or her son. Consequently, the boy, a model of humility, is forced to solicit help from others. When he succeeds in his solicitations, he thereby saves the life of his mother. The mawkish sentimentality of the book would make it unlikely reading for a child today; but, when it was published, one reviewer claimed that it was "a beautiful and affecting story, worthy of the authoress of *Redwood*."[61] In the nineteenth century, tales of virtuous children were enormously popular; for example, hundreds of thousands of copies of Martha Farquharson's *Elsie Dinsmore* (1867) were sold—the tale of a priggish young girl who, with biblical authority to back her up, disciplines herself to love Jesus more than her father. Susan Warner's bestselling *The Wide, Wide World* (1850) involves a pious child who devotes part of each day to prayer and the contemplation of Christian doctrine. Miss Warner clearly thought that little girls should be humble, pious, and docile — but so did most of the other authors who wrote books for children.

The warm reception which *The Deformed Boy* received may have encouraged Miss Sedgwick to write more children's books; in any case, she became a fairly prolific author of sketches and tales for the young; and some of her didactic tales were explicitly directed at a juvenile audience.

CHAPTER *4*

The Captive Unredeemed

It hath been deservedly esteemed one of the great and wonderful works of God in this *last age*, that the Lord stirred up the spirits of so many thousands of his servants, to leave the *pleasant land* of England, the land of their *nativity*, and to transport themselves, and families, over the *ocean sea*, into a *desert land* in America, at the distance of a *thousand leagues* from their own country; and this, merely on account of *pure and undefiled Religion*, not knowing how they should have their *daily bread*, but trusting in God for *that*, in the way *of seeking first the kingdom of God, and the righteousness thereof*: And that the Lord was pleased to grant such a gracious *presence* of his with them, and such a *blessing* upon their undertakings, that within a few years a *wilderness* was subdued before them. . . .

—John Higginson[1]

O NE of the most sensational of early American historical romances dealing with Puritan New England was the first novel of the editor, reformer, historian, poet, and, of course, novelist, Lydia Maria Francis Child. Mrs. Child—then Miss Francis—appears to have read Sir Walter Scott's *Waverly* almost as soon as an American edition was available. She was "greatly excited, and she exclaimed as she laid down the book, 'Why cannot I write a novel?' "[2] Indeed, although she was only twelve at the time, she was sufficiently impressed with this "versatile and daring genius" to produce within the following years a sensational historical romance filled with strange passion and unrequited love, *Hobomok: A Tale of Early Times* (1824), which also introduced a truly "noble savage" to the history of Puritan New England.[3]

The year 1826 saw the publication of the two-volume

[72]

Peep at the Pilgrims, the work of Harriet Vaughan Cheney, daughter of the early sentimentalist, Hannah Foster. Mrs. Cheney sympathetically regarded her forefathers as champions of "civil and religious freedoms."[4] The list of novelists who added to the growing debate about the worth of the American Puritans is seemingly endless; but, in mentioning only a few we would include John Greenleaf Whittier in *Margaret Smith's Journal* (1849), James Fenimore Cooper in *The Wept of Wish-ton-Wish* (1829), Nathaniel Hawthorne in *The Scarlet Letter* (1850), and Sir Walter Scott in *Peveril of the Peak* (1822).[5]

I *The Historian*

Hope Leslie (1827), Miss Sedgwick's third novel and her best, was based on her close study of colonial New England history as related by John Winthrop, William Hubbard, Cotton Mather, and John Trumbull. The novel is set primarily in New England, although the opening incidents take place in England. William Fletcher decides to go to America, where he will be free to practice his own religious beliefs. Upon his arrival in New England, Mr. Fletcher moves to the infant colony of Springfield, Massachusetts, where he settles with his wife, his infant son, and his older son Everell. Shortly afterwards, Hope and Faith Leslie, the daughters of an English friend, arrive in this country; and Mr. Fletcher, who is in Boston at the time of their arrival, sends Faith, the younger girl, to his home near Springfield. Also living in this house are Magawisca and Oneco, children of the Indian sachem Mononotto, who are held captive and who do the work of servants. When their father attacks the Fletcher home, he kills Mrs. Fletcher and her infant; and he takes Everell and Faith as his captives. He later tries to kill Everell with a tomahawk, but Magawisca intervenes at the last moment, and the tomahawk cuts off her arm.

The rest of the novel takes place several years later, and most of it is set in the colonial city of Boston where Hope Leslie and Everell are living. They number among their friends some of the most distinguished residents

of the city, some of whom—like John Winthrop—Miss
Sedgwick drew from historical accounts. On the other
hand, Faith Leslie has remained among the Indians, where
she has forgotten the English language, has been converted
to Catholicism, and has married Oneco. With the help of
Magawisca, Hope Leslie is reunited with her sister in a
secret meeting: but, during this meeting, Sir Philip Gardiner, the villain of the novel, captures Magawisca, whom he
charges with being an enemy of the Puritan Common-
wealth. Consequently, she is put on trial. Sir Philip, however, is only trying to gain the confidence of the Puritan
leaders; for he is secretly in league with men who would
like to undermine the political authority of the colony.
In addition, Sir Philip also has designs on Hope Leslie,
whom he plans to abduct and force to be his mistress.
His schemes fail, however, and he is killed when the
ship on which he is staying blows up in Boston harbor.
Meanwhile, Hope Leslie is able to arrange for Magawisca's escape from prison; and Magawisca joins the rest
of her family as they retreat from the civilized portions of
the colony and journey westward into the wilderness.

The subplot involves Esther Downing's love for Everell Fletcher. Hope Leslie is also in love with Everell;
but, feeling that he reciprocates Esther's love, she hopes
that they will be happy together. Later, however, it is
revealed that he loves Hope, not Esther. With Mr. Fletcher's consent, Hope and Everell are married, and the novel
ends.

Monotto, Magawisca, and Oneco are Pequod Indians;
and for information on this tribe, Miss Sedgwick consulted
William Hubbard's *Narrative of the Indian Wars in New
England,* which she supplemented with John Trumbull's
Complete History of Connecticut and John Winthrop's
Journal, which had been made available to the public in
1825 for the first time. On the other hand, she drew details
from Cotton Mather's *Magnalia Christi Americana,* including
a description of Winthrop which she quoted in part in the
novel:

Our New-England shall tell and boast of her *Winthrop,* a *law-
giver* as patient as *Lycurgus,* but not admitting any of *his* criminal

disorders; as devout as Numa, but not liable to any of *his* hea-
thenish madnesses; a governor in whom the excellencies of *Christianity* made a most improving addition unto the *virtues*, wherein,
even without *those*, he would have made a *parallel* for the great
men of *Greece* or of *Rome*, which the pen of a *Plutarch* has eter-
nized.[6]

But if Miss Sedgwick, like Mather, wrote of a noble
Winthrop and of "the Wonders of the Christian Religion,
flying from the deprivations of Europe, to the American
Strand," she was also quite close to Mrs. Child in presenting
pictures of native tribes who were somewhat different
from Mather's "barbarous Indians . . . , whose whole *religion* was the most explicit sort of *devil-worship*."[7] Contrary to Miss Sedgwick's account, the Pequod tribe, "that
great, spirited, and warlike nation," had caused the Puritan settlers unaccountable, and generally unprovoked,
sufferings.[8] The resulting war between the two peoples all
but obliterated the Pequod tribe, once the terror of all
other natives, as well as the Puritans, in the colony.

Unquestionably, the war was one of the bloodiest and
cruelest in early New England history; and it is no credit
to the English that they made the Narragansetts, under
Uncas, their allies. If we read that the Pequods tortured
their captives by cutting "large gashes in" their flesh
and then pouring "embers and live coals into their wounds,"
we can also find accounts of such Narragansett tortures
of the Pequods as when they, "kindling a large fire, violently tore [the captive] from limb to limb. Barbarously
cutting his flesh in pieces, they handed it round from one
to another, eating it, singing and dancing around the fire,
in their violent and tumultuous manner."[9]

The colonists' attack on the Pequods' Mistic fort mentioned
in *Hope Leslie*, occurred on May 26, 1637, and was followed on July 13 by the Great Swamp Fight, also mentioned in the novel. Of the second battle, Hubbard states
that the English quietly came upon the Indians, "sitting
close together, upon whom they discharged their pieces
loaden with ten or twelve pistol bullets at a time, putting
the muzzles of their pieces upon the boughs within a few
yards of them."[10]

With some of his best fighters, including Mononotto, Sassacus, the chief sachem of the Pequods, fled to the Mohawks to seek protection. The Mohawks, however were not willing, of course, to protect those who had been the terror of their land; and they attacked them, killing all but one; Mononotto, although wounded, managed to escape and then, conveniently for *Hope Leslie*, disappeared from the pages of history. In his journal, Winthrop recorded the incident in the following manner: "Mr. Ludlow, Mr. Pincheon, and about twelve more, came the ordinary way by land, and brought with them a part of the skin and lock of hair of Sassacus and his brethren, and five other Pequod sachems, who, being fled to the Mohawks for shelter, with their wampam . . . were by them surprised and slain, with twenty of their best men. Mononottoh [sic] was also taken, but escaped wounded."[11] (The scalp of Sassacus, incidentally, is described rather vividly in *Hope Leslie*.)

In addition to a history of the Pequod war, the historians of the Puritan colony included a note on the wife of Mononotto, who, says the Hubbard version,

with her children submitted herself, or by chance of the war fell into the hands of the English . . . she was in special recommended to the care of that honorable gentleman Mr. Winthrop, at that time being the worthy Governor of Massachusetts; who taking notice of her modest countenance and behavior, as well of her only request (not to suffer wrong either to the honor of her body or fruit of her womb) gave special charge concerning her, according to his noble and christian [sic] disposition.[12]

From this reference to the children of Mononotto grew the background for the stories in *Hope Leslie* of Oneco and his sister, Magawisca. Miss Sedgwick may have drawn on any one of a number of histories of the Puritan colony; but, in particular, she used Winthrop's for information about various other historical figures and incidents which are mentioned in passing—the founding of Springfield, William Pyncheon, Thomas Morton, the Reverend John Eliot, and so forth.

Hope Leslie is not entirely an accurate picture historically of early New England.[13] Miss Sedgwick's "noble savages," for example, are very much the creation of her own imagination; for there are few surviving records of the Puritan epoch which suggest that the savages were fully as noble as they appear to be in the novel. Miss Sedgwick does note, however, that Roger Williams once stated that "for the temper of the brain in quick apprehensions and acute judgments, to say no more, the most High and Sovereign God hath not made the Indian inferior to the European."[14]

In addition to reading Puritan history, Miss Sedgwick may have drawn upon various traditions in both her town and her family for *Hope Leslie*. For example, Magawisca's sacrifice for Everell, in which she loses her arm, may have been suggested by an episode in "Mumbet's" life. When "Mumbet" was still one of Colonel John Ashley's slaves, Mrs. Ashley had tried to punish "Mumbet's" sister, who was also one of his slaves, by striking her with a shovel. When "Mumbet" intervened, she took the full blow on her arm; and she apparently never regained full use of it. Also, Miss Sedgwick may have known of the attack made by Indians on a Stockbridge family in the summer of 1775—an attack resembling in some respects the one on the Fletcher home in the novel. A lone traveler coming upon the Stockbridge home of a Mr. Chamberlain saw an Indian emerging from the doorway with what proved to be a three-year-old child. The Indian, finding himself discovered, murdered the child and then fled. When the traveler entered the house, he "saw an infant taken from its cradle, and its brains dashed out against the mantle by another Indian, who also fled, while . . . a hired servant . . . had fallen in defending Mrs. Chamberlain, and lay upon the floor nearly dead with his wounds."[15] The father, who had thought only of his own safety, had hidden himself when the Indians had first arrived. Likewise, in *Hope Leslie* one of the servants hides and does nothing to protect the Fletcher family during the attack.

The Mohawks, who provided the greatest threat to the Berkshire countryside, appeared ready more than once to launch a full-scale attack on Stockbridge and the area around it. One incident which Miss Sedgwick relates in her autobiography occurred when the cry went through the town that "the Indians are coming!" The Dwight family took their daughter Pamela—Miss Sedgwick's mother— and fled to Great Barrington to escape what they believed was an imminent massacre. As it turned out, the alarm was false; but the feeling of terror that swept through the town when the first cry was heard was long remembered.[16]

Stockbridge was a community saturated with Indian history, and it is surely not surprising that, in the course of *Hope Leslie*, Miss Sedgwick made much use of the Housatonic Indians and their grand council meeting place, Laurel Hill, rising on the north from the banks of the Housatonic River near the Sedgwick home. But there was also something in the history of Miss Sedgwick's family which may have had a greater influence on the final form of *Hope Leslie* than the traditions and stories of the Housatonics, Mohawks, and Pequods that she had heard and read. This was the tale of Eunice Williams, the unredeemed captive who became almost a legend in the annals of colonial America.

II *The Massacre and Eunice Williams*

In the summer of 1821, Miss Sedgwick went on a journey to Canada and Niagara Falls with a party that included her brothers Robert and Theodore. Near the end of June, they reached Oneida, New York, the location of a reservation for the Iroquois Confederacy; and Miss Sedgwick wrote home of an Indian missionary there,

who presides over the spiritual interests of the poor natives. He is a far-away cousin of ours. . . . He is descended from a daughter of a Parson Williams, of Deerfield. She was taken by the savages during one of their incursions into the newly-formed [*sic*] settlement of our pious ancestors. She was so young that she soon lost all recollection of her parents. Many years after, when peace was established with our wild neighbors . . , her friends made a fruitless effort to recover her. She had married an Indian, and chosen his country for her country, and his God for her God . . . . Mr. Williams (for he bears the name of his maternal ancestors) is said to labor with great zeal and some success among the remnant of his tribe.[17]

The missionary to whom Miss Sedgwick refers was in all probability Eleazar Williams, who, according to some, was Eunice's great-grandson.[18] Miss Sedgwick's great-grandfather, Ephraim Williams, was the cousin of the Reverend John Williams, Eunice's father, the one-time minister of Deerfield, Massachusetts, and the author of *The Redeemed Captive Returning to Zion*, one of the most famous of the Indian captivity narratives. The Reverend Williams' autobiographical account begins with the Indian massacre of Deerfield—"On Tuesday the 29th of February, 1703-04, not long before the break of day, the enemy came in like a flood upon us; our watch being unfaithful"—and continues to the experiences of those captured by the Indians and the ultimate return of most to "Zion."[19] Within the account, however, is an incident which would have appeared especially sensational to the Puritan colonists—the fact that Williams' daughter, Eunice, had been prevented from returning and was still living with the enemy. "Oh! that all who peruse this history," wrote Williams, "would join in their fervent requests to God, *with whom all things are possible*, that this poor child, and so many others of our children who have been *cast upon God from the womb*, and are now *outcasts ready to perish*, might be gathered from their dispersions, and receive *sanctifying grace* from God."[20]

But Williams' daughter, who had been taken from the colony when only seven, was never to be redeemed. Instead, she, like Faith Leslie, soon forgot the English language, assumed the new name of Marguerite, and adopted the Catholic religion. She then married a Catholic Indian who had taken the name of either Francois Xavier Aronsen or John de Rogers, depending on which account is read; and she finally adopted an Indian way of life. Attempts were made to bring her back to New England; but, with the exceptions of three short visits in 1740, 1741, and 1761, she never returned.[21] The daughter of Parson

Williams, says one account of her life, "became the most
celebrated captive of the century, a romantic figure of
the frontier."[22] The "legend" of Eunice Williams was,
in turn, passed down to Miss Sedgwick, who gave it a
position of central importance in the story of Faith Leslie in the novel.

III History in Romance

Miss Sedgwick wrote in her Preface that "the following
volumes are not offered to the public as being in any degree an historical narrative, or relation of real events.
Real characters and real events are, however, alluded to;
and this course, if not strictly necessary, was found very
convenient in the execution of the author's design, which
was to illustrate not the history, but the character of the
times."[23]

Miss Sedgwick might have agreed with the thunderously
romantic proclamations of Miss Electa F. Jones: "the
descendants of Puritans . . . are calling upon streams
and upon lightning to aid them in the commemoration
of their ancestors; and they who at first bade this wilderness 'blossom as the rose,' and others who have continued
its culture, should not be forgotten, even though the
sand has for a time been blown over their footprints, and
the sods of their own beloved valley has [sic] covered
them."[24] But, at the same time, Miss Sedgwick was somewhat more critical of the Puritan than was the school of
Electa Jones and Harriet Cheney.

Miss Sedgwick also, while she could not overlook all
the wrongs committed by the Indians, could sympathize
more than Miss Jones with those who sought "the most
secluded and wildest spots, where the face of nature yet
untouched by man, expresses some sympathy for them—
owns an alliance with them"[25] Her ability to see both sides
leads to a more interesting picture both of those who
"though conquered, . . . were never enslaved," and of
the Puritans themselves who lived in settlements that,
in true melodramatic style, were "illuminated spots, clear
and bright lights, set on the border of a dark and turbu-
lent wilderness."[26]

IV *The Border of the Wilderness*

The narrative structure of *Hope Leslie* is the best of all the Sedgwick novels. The opening chapters involve, for example, a realistic and convincing narrative progression from a society of refined English gentlemen to the early settlement at Boston, then to a colonial outpost, and finally to an Indian encampment in the wilderness. William Fletcher, who possesses, like other Sedgwick heroes and heroines, "a disinterested love of his species," is the nephew of a wealthy English country gentleman and lawyer who considers the Puritans "seditious" and "mischief-brewing."[27] "One inquiry should suffice for a loyal subject," he says; " 'what is established?' and that being well ascertained, the line of duty is so plain, that he who runs may read."[28] He dismisses the Puritan preacher John Eliot as "a fanatical incendiary."[29] Fletcher is in love with his uncle's daughter Alice but also has fallen under the influence of Eliot and Eliot's friend, John Winthrop. The uncle forbids marriage unless Fletcher changes his religious views, but Fletcher decides that his religious principles are of greater importance than his happiness. The daughter is married to Charles Leslie; and in 1860, after having married an orphan who has been placed in Winthrop's care, Fletcher sails to America on the *Arabella*.

Of Fletcher and others like him, Miss Sedgwick, reflecting in part her readings of Cotton Mather and John Winthrop, states that "the magnitude of the enterprise in which the first settlers of New-England were engaged, the terrific obstacles they encountered, and the hardships they endured, gave to their characters a seriousness and solemnity, heightened, it may be, by the severity of their religious faith."[30]

Several years after his arrival in Boston, Fletcher decides to join Pyncheon, Holioke, and Chapin in their effort to found the community of Springfield on the banks of the Connecticut River. Fletcher, however, does not build his home in the community itself but a mile away, thereby placing himself, of course, on what was then the border of civilization; and he names his one-house settlement Bethel.

The border of the river was fringed with all the water-loving trees; but the broad meadows were quite cleared, excepting that a few elms and sycamores had been spared by the Indians, and consecrated by tradition as the scene of revels or councils. The house of our pilgrim was a low-roofed modest structure, containing ample accommodation for a patriarchal family; where children, dependants, and servants were all to be sheltered under one roof-tree. On one side . . . lay an open and extensive plain; within view was the curling smoke from the little cluster of houses about the fort—the habitation of civilized man; but all else was a savage howling wilderness.[31]

A letter arrives stating that Alice's husband is dead and that she has come to New England with her two children, and Fletcher is asked to care for them. Likewise, news is received that John Winthrop has obtained two Indians to be servants for the Fletchers. These are, of course, Oneco and Magawisca, the children of Mononotto, a sachem of the defeated Pequods. Fletcher goes to Boston where he stays with Alice's daughter Hope Leslie; and he sends her sister Faith, Magawisca, and Oneco to his home in the wilderness where they live with his wife, son Everell, three daughters, a baby boy, and their servants.

The narrative which precedes the Indian attack on Fletcher's wilderness home is a masterpiece of suspense. Carefully built from the moment that Mrs. Fletcher writes to her husband about the news of Indians in the area, the action slowly builds from the warnings of nearby residents and the strange, inexplicable actions of Magawisca—who is aware of the impending disaster—to the nights in which the Pequods can be sensed waiting in the forest and finally to the day of the attack itself. Miss Sedgwick's progress as a storyteller from *A New-England Tale* to *Hope Leslie* has been a rapid and successful one.

Two opposing views of the Pequod War are related shortly before the attack on Fletcher's home. One of his servants expresses the view found in the histories which Miss Sedgwick consulted; on the other hand, Magawisca relates the story of a purposeless slaughter of her people, including her brother, Samoset, who was beheaded for refusing to aid the English. As she tells it, her tribe—which the English considered "fierce, cruel, and war-like"— would have lived peacefully with the colonists if it had not been for their chief sachem, Sassacus, who was driven to destroy those who, he believed, were robbing him of his lands.[32] Magawisca's father, Mononotto, we are told, was "adverse to all hostility, and . . . was the advocate of a hospitable reception [for the English] and pacific conduct."[33]

Magawisca's interpretation has little basis in historical facts; but it adds to the conflict, illustrated in the novel, between the people of the wilderness and the people of civilization. Mononotto, who has seen his people massacred and his wife and children taken prisoner, has now turned from peace to revenge; and his first act is the destruction of Fletcher's home and family.[34] His desire for revenge results in the murder of Mrs. Fletcher and her infant son; and Everell, now fifteen, and Faith are taken prisoners and marched west to the Indian camping-grounds near what is present-day Stockbridge, Massachusetts.[35]

The events following the massacre were perhaps the most famous parts of the book when it was first published. Especially famous was the episode in which Magawisca sacrifices her arm on Laurel Hill—an actual location near Stockbridge—to save the life of Everell; but the episode is so excessively melodramatic that it would probably not affect most readers today in the same way that it affected readers a century and half ago when these incidents were widely known and wept over. Indeed, they made Laurel Hill something of a tourist attraction—so much so that when Mrs. Elizabeth F. Ellet wrote her guidebook, *Rambles about the Country*, some twenty years after the novel was published, she did not feel that it was necessary to give an exact description of the location of "sacrifice rock," since it seemed likely that most of her readers had been there already.[36] Even the Hawthornes visited Laurel Hill; and Melville paid a visit to the spot in the company of Oliver Wendell Holmes and the publisher James T. Fields.

V *Puritan and Indian*

Alexander Cowie wrote in *The Rise of the American
Novel* that in *Hope Leslie,* Miss Sedgwick "centres attention less on the action, however exciting, than on the
people: her books are not adventure stories."[37] Cowie
was correct; for, despite the novel's hairbreadth escapes
and flights through the wilderness, Miss Sedgwick was
far more interested in her characters and in what they
morally suggest. The characters are clearly divided into
three groups: the English, the Puritan colonists, and the
Indians.

Of the English characters in the novel, the most important is Sir Philip Gardiner; an arch-villain, he is a stock
figure borrowed from the sentimental novel. Like Mr. B. in
Samuel Richardson's *Pamela,* Sir Philip is characterized by
his sensual nature and his absolute lack of moral principle. He is "a man of the world, [practised] in all the arts
of society."[38] He is not a Puritan; but, as long as he is in
Boston, he finds it convenient to appear sympathetic to
the Puritan cause. In fact, he secretly desires to undermine and destroy the colony's government (history has
never revealed his exact reasons), and he is the "protégé
and ally of Thomas Morton, the old political enemy of the
colony."[39] Gardiner was probably suggested to Miss Sedgwick by a reference in Winthrop's *Journal,* where he is
known as Sir Christopher rather than as Sir Philip. "There
is no more singular and incongruous episode in the first
history of Massachusetts," wrote Charles Francis Adams
in *Three Episodes of Massachusetts History,* "save that
of the May-pole of Merry-Mount, than the episode of Sir
Christopher Gardiner. Who the man was, whence or why
he came, and whither he afterwards went, are matters
which have hitherto been wrapped in a mystery which is
not likely ever to be solved."[40]

Styling himself "Knight of the Golden Melice [*sic*],"
Gardiner arrived in the Massachusetts Bay Colony during
the first years of its settlement. He was a Catholic, but his
religious training did not prevent him from developing
a fairly complex married life; he had two wives (one in

London, one in Paris) and also a mistress. He returned
to England within a couple years and then joined Thomas
Morton and Ferdinando Gorges—two of the Puritans'
worst enemies—in a slanderous attack on the Massachusetts
Bay Colony. Then, instead of returning to America as
he does in *Hope Leslie*, he vanished from history. In
Hope Leslie, Gardiner is killed in the explosion of Captain
John Chaddock's ship in Boston harbor. History tells us
that this explosion actually occurred—Winthrop believed
that the ship was destroyed when "one striking fire
with a pistol, two barrells [*sic*] of powder took fire and
blew her up."[41] Miss Sedgwick was willing to change the
historical record when doing so suited her purpose. Gardiner's death on Chaddock's ship is, if not historically accurate, at least morally appropriate; for Miss Sedgwick's
villain, a man absolutely lacking in principles, receives an
especially grusome punishment.

It may be worth noting here that, according to Winthrop,
the ship's crew had been on shore before the explosion
took place and had consumed an especially large amount
of alcohol. Furthermore, "the captain and his master having
drank too much, the captain began to speak evil of the
country, swearing fearfully, that we were a base heathen
people."[42] Miss Sedgwick borrowed the historical drunken
sailors and described them in her novel; however, her
imagination added the Italian member of the crew who,
in his drunken stupor, decides that, if Hope Leslie is not
the Virgin Mary, she is surely "the blessed lady Petro-
nilla."[43] Once again Miss Sedgwick borrowed from history
but freely changed the record.

Sir Philip Gardiner is the only English figure to be
employed at any length in the novel, but some of the minor
characters are English, including one aristocratic, middle-
aged woman who maintains that whatever is "not practised
and known in England [is] not worth possessing."[44] Far
more interested in "the form of headpieces" than in religion, she is also "far more ambitious of being the leader of
fashion than the leader of a sect."[45] By contrast, Esther
Downing, one of the Puritans, is "disinterested, humble,
and devoted," "reserved, tender, and timid."[46] Miss Sedg-

wick unquestionably sympathized more with the Puritans than with the English; and yet, while she admired the courage of the Puritans in coming to America to practice their own religion, she felt that they lacked enthusiasm for life. This enthusiasm is what distinguishes Hope Leslie from Esther Downing and all the other Puritans. In one incident, we are told that "Hope Leslie, by rashly following her first generous impulses, by giving to 'unproportioned thought its act,' [had] effected that which the avowed tenderness of Miss Downing, the united instances of Mr. Fletcher and Governor Winthrop, and the whole colony and world beside, could never have achieved."[47]

It was probably Timothy Flint who reviewed *Hope Leslie* for *The Western Monthly Review* and criticized the character of Magawisca for being "the first genuine Indian angel." "This angel, as she stands," wrote Flint, "is a very pretty fancy; but no more like a squaw, than the croaking of a sand-hill crane is like the sweet, clear and full note of the redbird. Dealers in fiction have privileges; but they ought to have for foundations, some slight resemblance to nature."[48] Flint's characterization of Magawisca as an angel is a fitting one, but he failed to realize that the idealization of the Pequod maiden was quite intentional. Miss Sedgwick never intended her to be seen as one of Timothy Flint's realistic squaws; Magawisca is a "noble savage." She is, in fact, a Christian without the training of Christianity. She is good not because civilization has taught her to be so, but because her nature is to be charitable and kind. She would willingly sacrifice her life to save the life of someone else; in fact, she nearly loses her life in her attempt to save Everell Fletcher's. The Christian character, Miss Sedgwick suggests, has its origin in places other than ritual or doctrine.

Magawisca, we are told, possesses "the singular dignity and grace of . . . demeanor—a certain air indicating an 'inborn royalty of soul.' "[49] She dresses in a manner that has a "wild and fantastic grace" but that also harmonizes "well with [her] noble demeanor and peculiar beauty."[50] She remains a child of the forest—although surely no ordinary Indian squaw!

Faith Leslie could have been an interesting character, but she seldom appears in the novel; and Miss Sedgwick does little to characterize her. She is the unredeemed captive, who has entirely foresaken her Puritan background and accepted the nomadic life of an Indian. Faith is an anathema to the colonists; she is, says one Puritan, "a spoiled child . . . , and it seemeth a pity that the name of Faith was given to her, since her shrinking, timid character doth not promise, in any manner, to resemble that most potent of the Christian graces."[51] At the suggestion of Oneco, Faith adopts the Indian way of life and forgets the English language. Led by the teachings of a "Romish father," she, like Eunice Williams, becomes a Catholic—a rather horrifying conversion for strict Puritans.[52] Her marriage finally takes her away forever from the Puritan way of life. Quite different from the Faith described by the Puritan, she is now considered to be one with "an expression of gentleness and modesty," and her virtues are attributed to the teachings of the Indians— not to the teachings of the Puritans.[53] At the end of the book Faith decides not to return to Puritan civilization. She joins Mononotto and his children in "their pilgrimage to the far western forests. That which remains untold of their story," wrote Miss Sedgwick at the end of her tale, "is lost in the deep, voiceless obscurity of those unknown regions."[54]

VI *Hope Leslie*

In Adelheid Staehelin-Wackernagel's study, *The Puritan Settler in the American Novel,* she concluded that Hope Leslie "is a remarkable figure in the early novel. Her charm and liveliness are quite extraordinary for the time, and she is one of the truly attractive women in the whole range of portraits."[55] Unlike too many other women in early American novels, Cooper's in particular, Hope Leslie is a fully drawn, believable character. She combines two favorite Sedgwick characteristics: she is disinterested like most Puritans, she is also an enthusiast. Like Magawisca, Hope Leslie is a Christian not because the Puritan doctrines have taught her how a Christian should act; rather, she knows *instinctively* how a Christian should act. As much as she loves Everell Fletcher, Hope would rather see him marry Esther Downing if his doing so would make Esther happier. In all things, Hope considers her own happiness to be less important than that of others. Magawisca, of course, is also capable of impulsively doing the right thing. She appears much less frequently than Hope does, but morally she is in no way Hope's inferior.

Hope Leslie represents the high point of a characterization that begins with Jane Elton in *A New-England Tale* and continues with Ellen Bruce in *Redwood*: the characterization of the thoroughly virtuous woman. The characterizations of Jane Elton and Ellen Bruce are insufficient, since, as we have seen, Jane Elton is entirely incapable of defending herself; and there is reason to believe that, if Mr. Lloyd did not decide to marry her, she would remain at the mercy of a morally bankrupt society. On the other hand, Ellen Bruce is given little opportunity to prove her virtuous character. She is seen helping the sick and the poor and is said to be interested only in the welfare of others, but she does nothing which could raise her character to heroic stature. However, Hope Leslie, who possesses all of Jane's and Ellen's virtues, is confronted with a choice between doing what is legally right and doing what is morally right. She knows that Magawisca's imprisonment cannot be justified morally, for Magawisca is in no way the colony's political enemy that she is accused of being. However, there is no legal method for releasing the Indian maiden from the prison; therefore, Hope, doing what she knows is morally right, arranges for Magawisca's escape.

Miss Sedgwick's heroines in her novels after *Hope Leslie* are as insufficiently characterized as are Ellen Bruce and Jane Elton. Gertrude Clarence in *Clarence*, Isabella Linwood in *The Linwoods*, and Grace Herbert in *Married or Single?* are never given opportunities to prove their strength of character and virtue as fully as Hope Leslie does. Among Miss Sedgwick's portraits of virtuous women, the characterization of Hope Leslie is her most successful; and the characterization of Maga-

wisca may also be considered successful—if we are willing
to overlook Timothy Flint's complaint.

VII   *The Housatonic and the Hudson River*

Hope Leslie contains several descriptions of natural
scenery such as are found in Cooper's novels and in the
Hudson River School paintings of Thomas Cole and Asher
B. Durand. In these descriptions, the characters are
shown surrounded by a vast landscape as is the case in
Miss Sedgwick's description of the small Fletcher home
on the border of a vast wilderness. At one point in the novel,
Hope Leslie joins Mr. Fletcher and a friend in climbing
a mountain near Northampton, Massachusetts. Miss Sedgwick was thinking of Mount Holyoke, which afforded
magnificent views of the Connecticut River Valley,
and which was a major tourist attraction at the time *Hope
Leslie* was published. Indeed Mr. Fletcher's friend is Elizur
Holioke, a figure borrowed from history and the man
for whom Mount Holyoke was named.

From the summit of this mountain, Hope encounters
a landscape "that made me clap my hands, and my pious
companions raise their eyes in silent devotion."[56] Clearly
the landscape is more than a wilderness which must be
subdued and which hides the enemy Indians from the
Puritans. According to Hope, "he must have a torpid imagination, and a cold heart, I think, who does not fancy these
vast forests filled with invisible intelligences."[57] Miss
Sedgwick was neither a Pantheist nor a Transcendental-
ist, but she did not view landscape in purely esthetic or
economic terms. If, on the one hand, the Puritans were
confronted with a "howling wilderness," they were also
confronted with landscapes which were still in their pris-
tine state—landscapes which still looked very much as they
had when God created them. Consequently, while the
wilderness might hide an Indian behind every tree, wilderness landscapes had greater associations with God than with
men. No wonder then that when Fletcher and Holioke
first see the landscape from Mount Holyoke, they "raise
their eyes in silent devotion." When they look out over

the wilderness below them, they are looking, they believe, at the work of God.

Among Miss Sedgwick's contemporaries, James Fenimore Cooper made considerable use of the wilderness and its associations with the Deity. In *The Pioneers* (1823), for example, Cooper's hero Natty Bumppo speaks of a view from a mountain in the Catskills—a view encompassing "all that God had done, or man could do, far as eye could reach."[58] It is a view which includes "all creation."[59] According to Natty, "none know how often the hand of God is seen in the wilderness, but them that rove it for a man's life."[60] Natty, of course, opposes civilization and its destruction of the wilderness; therefore, as civilization pushes forward across the continent, he is continually forced to go westward. Natty has an intense love for wilderness; "the meanest of God's creatur's be made for some use, and I'm formed for the wilderness," he says; "if ye love me, let me go where my soul craves to be. . . . ."[61]

By contrast, much as Hope Leslie loves the wilderness, she chooses to live in Boston, the center of Puritan civilization. *The Pioneers* concludes with the tragic assumption that Natty's foe, civilization, will ultimately triumph over him and the wilderness he loves; however, *Hope Leslie* concludes with the marriage of the heroine to a successful Puritan in the city. She is the willing ally of civilization, and her descendants will be left with the task of settling the continent. However, Magawisca identifies herself as thoroughly with the wilderness as Natty Bumppo does; and, like Cooper's hero, she is unable to accept life in cities and towns. In the wilderness, "the Great Spirit, and his ministers," she says, "are every where present and visible to the soul that loves him; nature is but his interpreter; her forms are but bodies for his spirit." The wilderness is a moral teacher for Magawisca: she hears the voice of God "in the rushing winds—in the summer breeze—in the gushing fountains—in the softly running streams", and she sees Him "in the bursting life of spring—in the ripening maize—in the falling leaf."[62] As civilization advances, it destroys the wilderness; and *Hope Leslie* ends with the retreat of Magawisca and the remaining Pequods farther into the West.

VIII *Miscegenation*

Cooper's *The Last of the Mohicans* (1826) centers around two women, the half-sisters Alice and Cora Munro. Alice, a passive, withdrawn woman, requires the protection of the British Major Duncan Heyward. On the other hand, Cora is more courageous and self-reliant; and she is loved by two Indians: Magua, an enemy of the English, and Uncas, "the last of the Mohicans" who is sympathetic to the British cause. The novel's plot involves a series of adventures in the wilderness where Cora and Alice are first captured by Magua—who tries to force Cora to be his wife—and then are saved by Uncas and other friends of the English, including Cooper's hero Natty Bumppo. At the end of the novel, Heyward is united with Alice; but Cora, Magua, and Uncas are killed. D. H. Lawrence in his *Studies in Classic American Literature* (1923) concluded that Cooper morally could not allow marriage between Indians and whites; therefore, he killed off Cora, Magua, and Uncas to resolve his problem.[63] It is also strange that Cooper allowed the more pallid, shrinking, and withdrawn woman to survive but killed her more passionate, courageous, and self-reliant sister. The self-reliant woman receives only death; the passive woman lives happily ever after.

Hope Leslie was published a year after *The Last of the Mohicans,* and it is entirely possible that Miss Sedgwick's novel is in part an answer to Cooper's. Like Cooper, Miss Sedgwick contrasts two sisters—the self-reliant Hope Leslie and her passive, modest sister, Faith. Indeed, Hope and Faith resemble Cora and Alice, respectively. Cooper describes Cora as dark-skinned with black hair; Alice has a fair complexion. According to Miss Sedgwick, Hope has a rich complexion, a high color, and brown hair; her sister's face is colorless.[64] However, unlike Cora in *The Last of the Mohicans,* the self-reliant Hope is not killed at the end of the novel; it is she who is married to the hero. Furthermore, Miss Sedgwick permits miscegenation—the marriage of a white woman to an Indian—which Lawrence believed Cooper would never allow. Faith is, of course, married to Oneco, Magawisca's brother. Unlike

Cooper, Miss Sedgwick not only allows her courageous and self-reliant heroine to triumph but also permits marriage between Indians and whites.

Miss Sedgwick and her brothers were Abolitionists; and their father, as we have seen, was directly responsible for abolishing slavery in Massachusetts. Considering the racial tolerance practiced by the Sedgwick family, it should not be surprising that she chose an example of miscegenation from her own family history—the marriage of Eunice Williams to an Indian—as a central element in the story of *Hope Leslie*. Furthermore, Miss Sedgwick's portrait of her heroine as courageous and self-reliant, rather than passive like Cooper's Alice Munro, should be viewed in terms of her family background.

In the 1820's, it was most unusual for women to succeed professionally; a woman's place was quite literally in the home; and there were no opportunities for success in such traditional professions as law, medicine, and the ministry. However, within the Sedgwick family, there was as much opposition to restraints placed on a woman's professional objectives as there was to slavery. There is nothing in Miss Sedgwick's *Life and Letters* to suggest that she or any of her sisters-in-law or nieces were in any way like Cooper's passive and withdrawn heroine, Alice Munro.

IX *Sedgwick and Cooper*

James Fenimore Cooper and Catharine Maria Sedgwick were contemporaries, and both achieved substantial reputations as historical novelists and as novelists of manners. Beyond this point, however, they had little in common. Cooper was by far the more versatile and prolific writer; in the 1820's, he wrote novels about the Revolutionary War in New York State (*The Spy*, 1821), pioneer settlements (*The Pioneers*, 1823), life at sea (*The Pilot*, 1823), the Revolutionary War in Massachusetts (*Lionel Lincoln*, 1825), the wilderness (*The Last of the Mohicans*, 1826), the prairies (*The Prairie*, 1827), pirates (*The Red Rover*, 1827), Puritan history (*The Wept of Wish-ton-Wish*, 1829), and pirates again *(The Water Witch,* 1830). During the same decade, Miss Sedgwick published only four novels, two concerning contemporary New England *(A New-England Tale* and *Redwood),* one concerning Puritan history *(Hope Leslie),* and one concerning the aristocracy of New York City *(Clarence).*

Clearly the more prolific and versatile Cooper generally selected subjects quite different from Miss Sedgwick's, but other differences exist between the respective novels of the two writers. Cooper's novels center around men— Natty Bumppo in *The Pioneers, The Last of the Mohicans,* and *The Prairie;* Harvey Birch in *The Spy;* and so forth. His novels never center primarily on women—or "females" as he often calls them—and, as we have seen, he had a decided preference for passive rather than self-reliant women. On the other hand, Miss Sedgwick's novels all center on women, some of them passive like Jane Elton and Ellen Bruce and others entirely self-reliant like Hope Leslie and Magawisca. Cooper's interests were very largely antipodal to Miss Sedgwick's. They wrote during the same decades and achieved their fame in the same genre, but even when they treated the same subject— for example, the ideal woman—they treated that subject very differently.

In later decades Cooper's works bore even less similarity to Miss Sedgwick's; for he, of course, continued as an author of novels, while she became a writer of didactic tales. However, in any survey of the American novel, Miss Sedgwick's novels must be given attention beside Cooper's; in her portrayals of women as well as in her sketches of New England history, scenery, characters, and customs, she offers much in subject matter and in style that is not available in his works.

X *Matters of Style*

"Cooper's word-sense," wrote Mark Twain in "Fenimore Cooper's Literary Offenses" (1895), "was singularly dull." According to Twain, Cooper's ear "was satisfied with the *approximate* word"; for example, in *The Deerslayer* "verbal" is used instead of "oral," "unsophisticated" instead of "primitive," "brevity" instead of "celerity," and so forth.[65] Twain also considered Cooper's prose to be wordy; and to prove it, he took three paragraphs from *The Deerslayer* and showed how one hundred of their three hundred and twenty words were unnecessary, "wasted by the generous spendthrift."[66] Twain believed that all writers should "employ a simple and straightforward style"—something which Cooper demonstrably did not do.[67]

In contrast to Cooper's prose style, Miss Sedgwick's is "simple and straightforward"; she uses comparatively few modifiers and dependent clauses. She seldom uses the passive voice, and she avoids the baroque complexity of such sentences as the following from *The Last of the Mohicans:* "notwithstanding this apparent adherence in Magua to the original determination of his conquerors, Heyward could not believe his tempting bait was so soon forgotten; and he knew the windings of an Indian path too well to suppose that its apparent course led directly to its object, when artifice was at all necessary."[68] In contrast, the following passage from *Hope Leslie* is typical of Miss Sedgwick's prose:

The storm continued for the space of an hour, and then died away as suddenly as it had gathered. In another hour, the guard had safely landed at the wharf, and were conveying their prisoners to the Governor. He, and his confidential counsellors, who had been awaiting at his house, the return of their emissaries, solaced themselves with the belief that all parties were safely sheltered on the island; and probably would remain there during the night. While they were whispering this conclusion to one another, at one extremity of the parlour, Everell sat beside Miss Downing, in the recess of a window, that overlooked the garden. The huge projecting chimney formed a convenient screen for the lovers. The evening was warm—the windowsash thrown up.[69]

It is possible to find sentences in *Hope Leslie* which are as complex and baroque as Cooper's, and there are passages in his works which are written in as straightforward a style as Miss Sedgwick's. However, in the majority of instances, a reader can distinguish between the elaborateness of his style and the simplicity of hers. That simplicity became even more marked, incidentally, in her later didactic tales. Since she realized that her audience would include many children and poorly educated laborers, she purposely wrote in a style which was even simpler and more straightforward than that in *Hope Leslie* and her other novels.

XI *The Critics*

Hope Leslie, wrote Sarah Josepha Hale in *Woman's Record* (1853), "has continued to be [Miss Sedgwick's] most popular tale; and, indeed, no other novel written by an American, except, perhaps, the early work of Cooper, ever met with such success."[70] While some, like Timothy Flint, had objections to *Hope Leslie*, it was even more widely read and praised than *Redwood*. Even Frances Trollope, a Britisher with little love for anything American, had to admit that *Hope Leslie* was a "beautiful story" and had "great merit".[71] Discussing the effect of the novel on less critical readers, Donald Grant Mitchell in *American Lands and Letters* (1899) wrote that Miss Sedgwick's novel, thought by some to contain "pictures of savage life more truthful than those of Cooper," "rallied [for its author] a great army of admirers; and I can recall even now with vividness the great relish with which—more than sixty years ago—a company of school-boys in the middle of New-England, devoured its pages, and lavished their noisy sympathies upon the perils of 'Everell,' and the daring of the generous 'Magawisca.' "[72]

The historian Jean Charles Sismondi wrote from Switzerland to tell Miss Sedgwick how pleased he was with *Hope Leslie*, and the English authoress Mary Russell Mitford wrote that "your novels and those of Cooper will make American literature known and valued in England."[73] Lydia Howard Huntley Sigourney, an enormously popular poet of the time, devoted one of her poems to Stockbridge, *Hope Leslie*, and Miss Sedgwick—who, she said, "Hath moved her country's heart,/ And bade, from dim oblivion's trance,/ Poor Magawisca start;/ [and] Hath won a fame, whose blossoms rare,/ Shall fear no blighting sky. . . ."[74] *The North American Review*, a Unitarian journal which had approved of all Miss Sedgwick's writings since she attacked the Calvinists in *A New-England Tale*, declared that *Hope Leslie* was "the last of this lady's three larger works, and, in our judgment, the best."[75] Claiming that Miss Sedgwick was the first to portray successfully the early settlement of the country, the reviewer concluded his article by saying that "our author . . . , if the truth must be told, appears to entertain a decided partiality for her own sex. Nor can we blame her for it. We are in no humor, indeed, to find fault with her at all, or for anything."[76] Twenty years later, in an article which criticized John Lothrop Motley's *Merry-Mount*, one of this journal's anonymous reviewers stated that, "though a multitude of attempts have been made, the only successful novel we remember, founded on the early history of Massachusetts, is Miss Sedgwick's *Hope Leslie*."[77]

XII *The Family*

Miss Sedgwick's brothers continued to encourage her to write, and they acted as her literary agents. Robert was especially encouraging and helpful; and, shortly after the favorable reviews of *Hope Leslie* began to appear, she wrote to him that "it is fair that you should share whatever of praise is bestowed—you, the faithful usher and godfather of my little 'Hope'."[78]

Miss Sedgwick always valued praise from her brothers and other members of her family far more highly than she valued praise from her readers and critics. Her emotional dependence on her family increased in the years which followed the publication of *Hope Leslie*. She also became increasingly convinced that a woman's happiness depended heavily on whether or not she was married. "From my own experience," Miss Sedgwick wrote in the spring of 1828, "I would not advise any one to remain unmarried."[79] Although she later wrote *Married or Single?* to illustrate her belief that marriage was not always essential to a woman's happiness, she continued to award marriage to her heroines. Meanwhile, she visited frequently at Robert's home in New York; spent much time in Stockbridge, where both Henry and Theodore were now living; and maintained her own suite of rooms in Charles' home in Lenox.

CHAPTER 5

Court Circles of the Republic

Captain Hall, when asked what appeared to him to constitute the greatest difference between England and America, replied, like a gallant sailor, "the want of loyalty." Were the same question put to me, I should answer, "the want of refinement."

—Frances Trollope[1]

I *The Questions of Taste*

FOR twenty-one years, Captain Basil Hall participated in various explorations of uncivilized parts of the world undertaken by the British Navy. He used these travels as the bases for books which were quite popular in their day and which made him something of a minor celebrity. After retiring from the navy, he decided to undertake an exploration of his own, but he chose one which could hardly have been more dangerous—at least to his American reputation. In 1827 with his wife, he decided to travel through North America and, in the manner then becoming popular, to publish his observations. Like Mrs. Trollope after him, he was doomed from the moment he first reached for his notebook; for enlightened Americans could not endure presumptuous Englishmen who found little to praise in democratic America.

Although Miss Sedgwick maintained an aristocratic demeanor, and although she treated her social inferiors with marked condescension, she continued to believe that the democratic experiment would prove successful ultimately; therefore, she too had little love for those Englishmen who claimed that democracy in America was a failure. She believed that social distinctions in America were largely the result of differences in manners and that, contrary to what the British were saying, these differences would soon be eliminated. Unlike Basil Hall and Mrs. Trollope, Miss Sedgwick envisioned an approaching American Utopia endowed with unlimited social grace.

Basil Hall and his wife were among the many English travelers who visited the Sedgwick family in the Berkshires. Miss Sedgwick's writings were widely known in England; and her brother Henry, who was now living in Stockbridge, had acquired international attention through his attempts to reform the common law. The Sedgwicks had become celebrities, and visitors to this country eagerly sought introductions to the family. If we accept Basil Hall's published account, he was quite satisfied with his introduction to the Sedgwicks and especially with their hospitality. "I was gratified in a very high degree," he wrote, "by making acquaintance with the accomplished author of several works of fancy—'Redwood,' 'Hope Leslie,' and others."[2] As for the people of Stockbridge, he discovered them to be "universally as kind and obliging as I had found their countrymen elsewhere."[3]

His wife's private correspondence, however, reflected a considerably different attitude. Of a Stockbridge gathering arranged for the pleasure of the self-appointed aristocrats, Mrs. Hall noted with contempt that "the party was evidently got together to stare at and listen to Basil."[4] "The Sedgwick family is of the greatest importance" in Stockbridge, Mrs. Hall told a friend in England, "and both males and females are more cultivated than most families, but I do not think any of them particularly agreeable except Miss Sedgwick."[5] After the visit, Captain Hall committed the supreme error in writing to Miss Sedgwick "criticising the style of her writings in the habitual tone of an Englishman."[6] Not surprisingly, Miss Sedgwick noted of Basil and his wife that, "as Americans, there is no love lost between us."[7]

Captain Hall is perhaps the Englishman caricatured as Mr. Edmund Stuart in Miss Sedgwick's fourth novel, *Clarence* (1830). In a footnote, the author remarks that "there may appear to be a striking coincidence between the opinions of our traveller and those announced in

Captain Basil Hall's travels; but no allusion was intended to those volumes."[8] But, while *Clarence* contains no allusions to the Englishman's book, Miss Sedgwick was careful not to mention that the figure of Edmund Stuart might be a picture of Captain Hall himself.

Such travelers as Stuart, says one of the central figures in *Clarence*, "come predetermined to find fault—to measure every thing they see by the English standard they carry in their minds, and which they conceive to be as perfect as those eternal patterns after which some ancient philosophers supposed the Creator to have fashioned the universe."[9] Stuart keeps a notebook in which he finds much reason to scribble, and Miss Sedgwick transcribes with obvious maliciousness one of the notebook's passages. "Justice U[pton] an abyss of ignorance—wife, a mighty vulgar little person—children, pests—no *servants*—two *helps*. Dined at Clarenceville. The C[larences] great people in America—giants in Lilliput!—Amer'n table barbarisms—porter and salad with meats! peas with currie!—no poultry—no butcher's meat. Query, do the inferior animals as well as man uniformly degenerate and become scarce in America?"[10]

Although there are many good—or at least interesting— passages in *Clarence* besides the Edmund Stuart episode, they comprise only a little space in the two volumes; as a result, the novel has little interest today for anyone but students of American literature. Unlike *Redwood* and *Hope Leslie*, both of which remain highly readable and entertaining works of fiction, *Clarence* is dated not only by its excessively melodramatic and sentimental plot but also by its concept of an ideal society, one derived from Jefferson's picture of an agricultural Republic in which talent and virtues are the most respected qualities.

The problems of an urbanized and industrialized Republic could hardly be solved quite so easily as Miss Sedgwick supposed. In *Clarence*, she envisioned an ideal society dominated by a cultured and at least moderately wealthy, rural gentry. When Mr. Clarence, a resident of New York City, inherits an enormous sum of money from his father, he—rather than use this money to better his position in society—moves to the country with his daughter Gertrude. Here he is the richest and most influencial man in the community of Clarenceville. Among his acquaintances is one Mrs. Layton, the mother of Emilie Layton, who shares with Gertrude Clarence a well-mannered charitable disposition. Unlike Gertrude's father, however, Mrs. Layton wishes to rise in society and would much prefer a fashionable life in New York City to a quiet life among rural gentry.

Consequently, Mrs. Layton is willing to marry her daughter to a man named Pedrillo, who is indeed very wealthy but who is also morally bankrupt. He abducts Emilie and attempts to seduce her; but, at the end of the novel, she is saved in a last-minute rescue. Meanwhile, Mr. Clarence has taught Gertrude to select her companions on the basis of their character, not their wealth. She is especially attracted to Gerald Roscoe, a respectable and morally upright man. However, Louis Seton, an artist, falls in love with her. Although she admires Seton's sincerity and his indisputably moral character, she knows that he lacks Roscoe's courage and decisiveness; consequently, she chooses to marry Roscoe. *Clarence* ends with Gertrude's marriage to Roscoe and Emilie's to Randolph Marion who helped save her from Pedrillo's villainy.

Miss Sedgwick's ideal aristocrats are Mr. Clarence and his daughter Gertrude who are wealthy, well read, and well traveled. Their learning is suggested by their library, which contains copies of the latest journals, *The North American Review,* the *London Quarterly,* the *Literary Gazette*—all of which have been studiously examined. Mr. Clarence and Gertrude, who are exquisitely well mannered, are capable of handling social emergencies with the utmost delicacy. Their travels include a journey to Trenton Falls, which an American of the time would have recognized as a resort virtually without equal. Niagara Falls might attract a wider cross section of Americans, but the upper classes never feared a lack of social equals at Trenton Falls.

Mr. Clarence and Gertrude are not, however, members

of the country's aristocracy of wealth, a fact which Miss Sedgwick, of course, felt was all for the good. Rich aristocrats, condemned on page after page of the novel, are characterized as people who have no more than money to justify their select social positions. While the Clarences do have wealth themselves—and a much greater wealth than most Americans of the time ever possessed—Mr. Clarence, true Jeffersonian that he is, insists that talents and virtue (and, one should add, good manners) are the only qualities which should be allowed to separate one class from another. The wealthy, he insists, compose only an artificial aristocracy, one which can exist merely at the whim of good, prosperous business. Some of the episodes in *Clarence* take place in New York City, where the ruling aristocracy is that of wealth. Here women are far more concerned with their dress than the extent of their reading, and they go to lectures to be seen rather than to learn. Miss Sedgwick clearly believed that women should devote their time to acquiring knowledge—which is exactly what her heroine does when she is in the country.

In order to insure that Gertrude is not corrupted by New York's rich and fashionable society—into which group her mother was born—Mr. Clarence removes her to the countryside where Gertrude will be free to develop her talents and virtues, read *The North American Review*, and become, in short, a lady. Gertrude does, indeed, become a lady but one who is, unfortunately, hardly more interesting or human than, for example, Alice Munro in Cooper's *The Last of the Mohicans*. Although Gertrude is—like Jane Elton, Ellen Bruce, and Hope Leslie—one of Miss Sedgwick's ideal women, she is not sufficiently substantial to hold the reader's interest. Her refusal or her inability—the reader is never sure precisely which—to be involved in anything that might be considered improper is so constant that the reader can conclude little more about her than that she is perfectly well mannered, nicely behaved, and decidedly dull!

In *Hope Leslie,* Miss Sedgwick's heroine proved the strength of her convictions when she helped Magawisca escape from prison; but Gertrude Clarence has no such opportunities to prove herself. According to one of the century's authorities on good behavior, "from the captain of a western steamboat to the roughest miner in California, from north, south, east and west, we hear but one voice. Women are to be protected, respected, supported and petted."[11] Gertrude is indeed "protected, respected, supported and petted" by her father; there is no reason to fear that she will ever be in a situation where her virtues will be fully tested. Gertrude Clarence will always live in a world comprised mainly of wealthy aristocrats with talents and virtues like her own.

The ideal, upper-class woman of Miss Sedgwick's day was not a very interesting person precisely because the range of her experience was considerably limited. She knew little of the world outside fashionable watering places and the homes of the country's aristocracy. This ideal woman was intensely well bred and virtuous, but there was little for her to do with her time. Furthermore, the country's relatively young aristocracy had not developed a complex system of manners such as Jane Austen used in her novels about the English nobility and the landed gentry. Miss Sedgwick wrote that Gertrude "was truly . . . a fit heroine for the nineteenth century; practical, efficient, direct, and decided . . ."and that ". . . she loved in moonlight and retirement, to abandon herself to visions of her imagination. . . ."[12] Practical and also romantic—the formula had worked in the creation of Ellen Bruce and Hope Leslie; but Gertrude is largely a model of proper manners for young ladies. Whether nursing the dying Louis Seton, trying to prevent Emilie's marriage to Pedrillo, or caring for her father, Gertrude is clearly "disinterested"—that is, she makes the welfare of others her first objective. As she explains to Mrs. Layton, she lives according to her principles, and charity is evidently the greatest of these. But Gertrude is never in a position where she might have to compromise her principles—where, for example, she might have to choose, as Hope Leslie does, between moral right and established law.

Some of the novel's more successful passages, especially

those in which Edmund Stuart and wealthy aristocrats are satirized, suggest that, had the author been more careful with the book's composition, *Clarence* could have been a successful novel of manners. Curiously, aside from various works by Cooper and Miss Sedgwick, very few good works of fiction were explicitly devoted to a study of manners in pre-Civil War America. To be sure, there are women who industriously wrote domestic novels in which much attention was given to manners. These novels included works by Maria Cummins, Susan Warner, Mrs. E. D. E. N. Southworth, and others, most of whom have been justly forgotten—but few authors of distinction attempted this particular kind of fiction. Perhaps the very lack of a class, or at least a highly influential class, which based its principles upon a life of manners precluded the possible development of a tradition of novels of manners in the half-century before the Civil War. Whatever the case, *Clarence* differs from most novels published in America at the time; and, in its occasional passages satirizing the wealthy aristocrats of New York, it appears to look forward to the kind of social satire with which Edith Wharton was to prove especially capable.

Unfortunately much of *Clarence's* plot and many of its characters owe little to Jane Austen, Maria Edgeworth, or other novelists of manners. *Bons vivants* (such as Pedrillo), chaste maidens (Emilie and Gertrude), a mad artist (Louis Seton), perilous escapes—*Clarence* contains them all. The plot includes not only an abduction but also an attempted seduction—and a happy ending. There are also comments on sensibility ("affairs of the heart") and sense ("affairs of the world"), but these subjects are treated so superficially that the reader who has not read Austen's *Sense and Sensibility* may wonder why the British novelist thought them worth an entire novel.

Miss Sedgwick claimed that *Clarence* "has something to do with every-day and present life," but the "every-day and present life" which she described in the novel was one with which few of her readers were acquainted.[13] Indeed, *Clarence's* popularity—and like most of Miss Sedgwick's works, *Clarence* was widely read—may be attributed in part to its concentration on the upper classes. At the least, the novel could have provided welcome escape reading for average Americans, those whose lives were decidedly less fashionable that Gertrude Clarence's.

II *The Family*

Clarence was dedicated "to my brothers—my best friends," and the dedication was signed, "Their Author." Miss Sedgwick relied on her brothers so thoroughly that she had good reason to sign the dedication to *Clarence* as she did. While Miss Sedgwick was writing *Clarence*, the first break in her family circle occurred. In 1827 or 1828, Henry Dwight Sedgwick suffered a mental breakdown. That caused him to give up his law practice in New York and move back to the family home in Stockbridge. Although he was well enough in the spring of 1831 to prepare his final work, *The Practicability of the Abolition of Slavery,* he spent most of his last years in periods of great depression and was occasionally fully unaware of the world about him. In December, 1828, Miss Sedgwick wrote of her brother: "to see a mind once so powerful, so effective, so luminous, darkened, disordered, a broken instrument—to see him stared at by the vulgar, the laugh of children—oh, it is too much! and yet his reason and his affections are struggling with this evil. His love seems an inextinguishable light; it shines through the darkness."[14] Nearly three years later, Miss Sedgwick wrote to one of her sisters that their brother had been able to speak but once during the past three days. His death occurred shortly afterward.

When *Clarence* was published, Miss Sedgwick was living part of the year in New York with her brother Robert and the rest in Lenox with her brother Charles and his wife, whom she described as a woman with "talents and enthusiasm to admire and appreciate."[15] In 1828, Charles' wife opened in Lenox a school for girls, which was to be "regarded as one of the best, if not the best, in the United States."[16] Among the students were a Delano, a Saltonstall, a Cushman, and a Marcy and others from the aristocracies of Boston and New York. In addition, there were several

students who later achieved fame in the arts; and among
these were Harriet Hosmer, once famed as a sculptress and
admired by Hawthorne, as well as Maria Cummins, whose
writings he did not admire but whose highly sentimental
novel *The Lamplighter* was an example of "best-sellerdom"
on a mammoth scale. Best known of Mrs. Sedgwick's students
was Jennie Jerome, who became the mother of Winston
Churchill.

Mrs. Sedgwick was also the author of several happily
forgotten volumes ranging from *The Beatitudes* to *A Talk
with My Pupils,* which includes advice on such subjects
as "Relations with Servants." On this particular theme,
Mrs. Sedgwick offers the following instruction: "much that
is trying in servants often proceeds from mere narrow-
mindedness; they can see only as those see who walk in
a dark night with a lantern, which throws the light a short
straight distance before them, so that they are quite blind
to anything bearing on their course that should induce
them to alter it. In such cases you must condescend, if
condescension it be, to reason with them, and endeavor to
enlighten them."[17] We can imagine Miss Sedgwick and
her sister-in-law looking over their estate in the Berkshires and discussing the problems of servants and their
lot in life—Mrs. Sedgwick creating tenets for her *Talk,*
and Miss Sedgwick outlining one of her books intended
to promote social reform—perhaps *Live and Let Live;
or, Domestic Service Illustrated.*

Meanwhile, another sister-in-law, Susan Anne Livingston Ridley Sedgwick, Theodore's wife and one of Miss
Sedgwick's closest friends since their days together at a
private school for young ladies in Albany, New York, was on
her way to becoming a successful purveyor of moral lessons
for the young—books similar in didactic treatment to
those Miss Sedgwick wrote for children. Mrs. Sedgwick's
Morals of Pleasure (rather innocuous and unexciting
pleasure) appeared in 1829; and soon she was rated highly
as a moral instructor for children.

Between the publication of *Clarence* (1830) and the
publication of *The Linwoods* (1835), Miss Sedgwick continued to contribute to magazines and annuals, saw some

of her shorter works anthologized, and prepared "Le Bossu," a story set in Charlemagne's France, for a collection of American works edited by Bryant and entitled *Tales of Glauber-Spa*. By this time, Miss Sedgwick's popular and critical reputation as a novelist had risen to perhaps its greatest height. Although she later acquired fame as an instructor of good morals and good manners, her fame as a novelist was probably never higher than during the mid-1830's. There were few critics during these years who did not include her with Cooper, Irving, and Bryant as one of the major figures in a rapidly growing American literature.

About this time Miss Sedgwick went to Washington, where Martin Van Buren, a family friend and then Vice-President, took her to the White House to meet President Andrew Jackson. Shortly afterward, she received a private call from Chief Justice John Marshall, who wrote home to his wife,

Who do you think I have seen? . . . I am sure you will not guess the person and I will therefore tell you without keeping you longer in delightful suspense. I have seen Miss Sedgwick, the author of Hope Leslie [*sic*]. I called on her today, a complement I pay very few ladies, and she thanked me for it. She is an agreeable, unaffected, not very handsome lady. . . . I was pleased with her and shall read her new work when I go home with the more pleasure for having seen her.[18]

III *Doing the War*

Miss Sedgwick's last major novel, aside from *Married or Single?* was *The Linwoods* (1835), the historical novel of the American Revolution. Although it contains some interesting characters and passages and is superior to *Clarence*, the romance is not a particularly good one and certainly not worthy of the generous praise that critics gave it in its day.

The novel centers on the Linwoods, a Tory family in New York, and on the Lees, a Republican family in New England. The families become acquainted with each other when Herbert Linwood goes to New England for his

schooling and boards in the Lees' home. Here he acquires
the Lees' Republican sentiments; and, when the Revolutionary War begins, he joins the colonists' Army and is
disowned by his father, who maintains an unswerving
trust in the British cause. Meanwhile, Bessie Lee has
gone to school in New York, where she has lived with the
Linwood family. Through the Linwoods, she has met Jasper
Meredith, a Tory, and has fallen in love with him. Meredith,
however, rejects Bessie's love—although he makes at first
a pretense of accepting it. He learns through his mother
that, since Mr. Linwood has disowned his son, Isabella
will inherit her family's fortune. Consequently, he deter-
mines to devote all his attentions to Isabella. Meredith's
rejection drives Bessie mad, and she disappears from her
home in New England and travels around the countryside in
search of him.

Bessie's brother, Eliot Lee, joins the colonists' army and
is stationed with Herbert Linwood at West Point. As a
messenger for General Washington, Eliot travels to New
York—the British stronghold—where he sees Isabella.
To round off the rather complex Romantic plot, he falls
in love with Isabella, while Herbert Linwood admits
his love for Eliot's sister Bessie! Herbert does not marry
Bessie, however; for, after recuperating from her mental
breakdown, she decides to live a single life. However,
at the conclusion of the war—and also of the novel—Eliot
is married to Isabella Linwood. Among the minor characters
in the novel is a Mrs. Archer, a relative of the Linwoods.
Several chapters in the middle of the novel involve an
attack by marauders on her family and her country home.
Her house is burned to the ground; but, in a last-minute
rescue, Eliot Lee saves her life and the lives of her children.

Miss Sedgwick had heard much about the Revolutionary
War from her father, who had fought in the Battle of White
Plains, New York; from the townspeople of Stockbridge;
and from family friends, including an elderly woman in
New York whose husband had been a hero in the American
cause. At the time Miss Sedgwick wrote *The Linwoods*,
the Revolution was less than sixty years in the past, and
many still lived who remembered the war. Unfortunately

for a novelist, however, their memories did not operate very critically; and, according to their descriptions, the American military leaders had been nothing short of divine. Miss Sedgwick believed all that she heard; and, whenever there was an opportunity in her novel, she introduced another one of the archangels—John Hancock, John Adams, Thaddeus Kosciusko, (Mad) Anthony Wayne, Israel Putnam, the Marquis de LaFayette, and Alexander Hamilton, the Honorable Theodore's own hero, who appears with "his face glowing with the sympathies and chivalric sentiment always ready to gush from his heart when its social spring was touched."[19] Even Colonel Ashley of "Mumbet" infamy is mentioned, and is credited with saying about Washington: "I venerate him next to the Deity."[20] Miss Sedgwick apparently shared the emotion, and she notes with much satisfaction that the General imitated God;[21] but, "whenever he could be so without the sacrifice of higher duties," Washington was "alive to the social virtues and affections."[22]

Against this backdrop, Miss Sedgwick places her central figures, none of them especially complex. One has "honest, heartfelt, constant affections" to elevate "the humblest and the meanest."[23] Another is given "the wound that rankled at her heart," "shattered faith," "blighted hopes," and "unrequited love."[24] One of Miss Sedgwick's objectives in the *The Linwoods* is to demonstrate the value of the common man; therefore, the book concludes with the marriage—the triumphant marriage—of one "fit to grace a peerage" with "the portionless son of a New-England farmer."[25]

With the exception of a few scenes in *Hope Leslie*, Miss Sedgwick maintained an unblemished record in her misuse of melodrama—Charles Dickens would have blushed to read her pages. The marauders' attack on Mrs. Archer's country home is outstanding in its unabashed use of melodrama and sentimentality. Miss Sedgwick places not only Mrs. Archer but also her two blind children at the mercy of heartless marauders who have come to steal money which, in fact, Mrs. Archer does not have. Furthermore, she is far from help of any sort; indeed, before help can arrive, the marauders have carried off one of the children; and the house has been set on fire. In addition, the child who is carried off is nearly killed; in fact, everyone believes that the child *is* dead, and only at the last minute, while plans are being made for a burial, does the child revive. Of her children, Mrs. Archer says, incidentally, "I have seen men with hard features and rough hands arrested by the sound of their voices, and as they listened, the tears trickling down their weather-beaten faces."[26] The Mrs. Archer episode does allow Eliot Lee to prove his bravery—it is he who saves her life and the lives of her children—but it remains loosely tied to the main plot involving the Linwoods and the Lees. The incident does allow Miss Sedgwick to make extensive use of sentimentality and melodrama—characteristics which, unfortunately, she could not avoid.

Readers in 1835 may not have objected to this novel's extensive melodrama and sentimentality; but, oddly enough, one reader was disturbed with its use of profanity—"d——d," "d——l," and so forth. When Miss Sedgwick visited the South Boston school of one Mr. Wells—a man who "from his childhood" had "loved boys"—he told her that he had read his students all of her books with the exception of *The Linwoods*; in that book, he explained, there were "some bad words, some profanity!" In all seriousness, Miss Sedgwick confided to her diary that this criticism was "worth remembering"; and she added that, in the second edition, she would correct, whenever possible, "this fault."[27]

IV *This Is My Father's World*

Miss Sedgwick's disagreement with the theology of Stephen West received another hearing in *The Linwoods*. However, by the time she came to write *The Linwoods*, the New England Calvinism which she criticized in *A New-England Tale* had ceased to be as threatening as it had seemed in 1822. Congregationalism with its strong Calvinistic emphasis had ceased to be Massachusetts' official state religion; and, among other Unitarian ministers, William Ellery Channing had been invited to preach in the Berkshires. Consequently, rather than directly attacking the Reverend West's concept of an unmerciful God and sinful man, she was satisfied with mocking gently his self-importance. Although she had noted once that one Calvinist preacher's "intemperate abuse" was "no more worthy of notice than the ravings of a Madman," she had so mellowed by the time she wrote *The Linwoods* that she portrayed the Reverend West in the character of the Reverend Wilson, an altogether harmless and likable, if theologically mistaken, gentleman.[28] Curiously, her dislike of Congregationalism had been replaced in part by an amused attitude toward its preachers:

Our good parson Wilson was an Apollo "in little"; being not more than five feet four in height, and perfectly well made,—a fact of which he betrayed the consciousness, by the exact adjustment of every article of his apparel, even to his long blue yarn stockings, drawn over the knee, and kept sleek by the well-turned leg, without the aid of garters. On entering Mrs. Lee's parlour, he gave his three-cornered hat, gold-headed cane, and buckskin-gloves [*sic*] to little Fanny, who, with the rest of the children, had at his approach slunk into a corner (they need not, for never was there a kinder heart than parson Wilson's, though somewhat in the position of vitality enclosed in a petrefaction), and then giving a general bow to the company, he went to the glass, took a comb from his waistcoat-pocket, and smoothed his hair to an equatorial line around his forehead; he then crossed the room to Mrs. Lee with some commonplace consolation on his lips; but the face of the mother spoke too eloquently, and he was compelled to turn away, wipe his eyes, and clear his throat, before he could recover his official composure.[29]

Miss Sedgwick's books are filled with portraits such as this one, but they become increasingly less successful in works after *The Linwoods* because of their sentimentality. When Miss Sedgwick wrote her autobiography, she created another portrait of Stephen West, one quite as detailed as the one in this novel but more successful, because less sentimental, than many of the portraits in her later writings.[30]

Sentimentality, melodrama, the American Revolution,

and Miss Sedgwick's name were in high demand in 1835; and, although *The Linwoods* sided with the American cause, even *The Athenaeum,* a British publication, gave it lavish praise; and Harriet Martineau, the imperious Briton, declared it to be "an advance upon *Hope Leslie.*"[31] *The North American Review,* a bastion of Unitarianism, was surely pleased to discover Calvinism being slighted once again; the journal called the book Miss Sedgwick's "most agreeable" novel; and Donald Grant Mitchell, alias "Ik Marvel," wrote at the turn of the century that *The Linwoods* "challenged attention, and held it, when *Woodstock* and the *Fair Maid of Perth* were still fresh from Abbotsford."[32] (Scott had died, however, three years before *The Linwoods* was published; *Woodstock* appeared in 1826; *Fair Maid,* in 1828.)

Unlike Cooper, Miss Sedgwick had much difficulty finding new plots and characters for her fiction. Thus she once again employed an ideal virtuous woman— Isabella Linwood—at the center of her narrative. Although Miss Sedgwick had discovered new ground for her fiction, she did not choose a new hero or heroine to complement the Revolutionary War setting; and, once again, she developed her narrative around a heroine whose central characteristics are faith, hope, and charity. Isabella Linwood is able to overlook political differences and to see the good both in her father, who sides with the Royalists, and in her brother, who fights for the American cause. She has faith that all things ultimately work out for the best and devotes herself to the welfare of others; indeed, one of the first things we learn about her is that she made the arrangements for Bessie Lee to come to New York where it would be possible for her to get a better education. Isabella's marriage to Eliot Lee at the end of the novel is symbolic of the new social order made possible by democracy; the son of a poor farmer is able to marry the daughter of a wealthy aristocrat.

The Linwoods was the last novel Miss Sedgwick published for more than twenty years. (Her next novel, *Married or Single?* was not published until 1857.) During the intervening years, she achieved an enormous popularity as the author of didactic tales for laborers and children. Unlike her novels, these works were clearly not directed at a sophisticated reading audience, and they did not receive the wide critical attention that had been given to her writings from *A New-England Tale* to *The Linwoods*. However, the didactic tales were very widely read and received much praise from those who were interested in social reform, but in general, although many critics did praise Miss Sedgwick's desire to upgrade society through her didactic tales, few continued to treat her as a novelist to be ranked with Cooper. This change in critical attitude is suggested by the slight condescension of the following passage from an article in *The North American Review:* "we noticed, not long ago, accounts in the newspapers of a meeting of female writers of this and other countries, at the residence of Miss Sedgwick, in Berkshire. If we were not misinformed by the daily chronicle of the times, Miss Sigourney, Mrs. Butler, Miss Martineau, Miss Gould, and we know not how many more of their fair compeers, were assembled upon this occasion, constituting a sort of female *wittenagemote*, or, in more intelligible language, a *Blue Congress*."[33]

CHAPTER 6

The Blue Congress

"Pshaw, Mr. Flint," said Mrs. Layton, "are you under the de-
lusion of imagining we go to the Athenaeum to see or to hear?"
"What do you go for, then?" honestly asked Flint.
"To be seen, my good friend—to fulfill our destiny, and be the
observed of all observers."

—Catharine Maria Sedgwick, *Clarence*[1]

I *Salvation through Reform*

I N the mid-1840's, Catharine Beecher wrote to Miss
Sedgwick to ask her to be one of a committee "to advance
her (Miss B's) philanthropic project for 'saving the country.'" As Miss Sedgwick told the educator Horace Mann,
"there are obvious difficulties acting in concert with Miss
B—and besides I do not understand what responsibilities
are incurred by consenting to become one of Miss B's
collaborateurs." She added, nonetheless, "I do not feel
at liberty to decline rendering any service in my power
in so great a cause."[2]

Since the "cause" was education, it was entirely logical
that Miss Beecher should enlist Miss Sedgwick's help; for she
was quite interested in education and taught for a while at the
Lenox school run by her sister-in-law, though she appears
never to have been deeply involved in this particular
project. Although none of her surviving letters mention
her work at the Lenox School, references to her teaching
appeared in the newspapers and other journals of the day.
Her friend N. P. Willis wrote that "original literature
in the lump is sadly at a discount in this country. Miss
Sedgwick, in the plentitude of her powers has taken to
school-keeping."[3] Although Willis thought that her time

would have been better spent writing books, it was only logical that she tried teaching as a profession. After all, her most widely read books after 1835 were didactic tales, which sought to teach manners and morals to children and to the lower classes. Furthermore, Miss Sedgwick was always interested in movements for social reform; and, since many attempts were made to reform education in mid-nineteenth century America, it should not have surprised anyone to find her using her sister-in-law's school to try out some of her own ideas on the subject.

Miss Sedgwick's interest in reform movements brought her numerous requests to sit on committees organized to correct social injustices. People like Catharine Beecher knew that it was very important to have highly respected figures engaged in reform movements; widely respected people like Miss Sedgwick could give even the most radical of these movements an air of respectability. Although one reviewer of one of her didactic tales was distressed to find in it "a tinge of *Radicalism*," most reviewers considered her didactic teachings merely good, sensible advice.[4] If the reviewers' opinion of Miss Sedgwick reflected the opinion of most readers, then leaders of reform movements could not have failed to see how valuable her participation could be.

There were few social reform movements which did not interest Miss Sedgwick; and, as we have already observed, she was directly involved in movements to improve the quality of education, to obtain rights for women, to abolish slavery, and to improve conditions in the prisons. Her family had always been involved with "causes"—especially the abolition of slavery—and Miss Sedgwick, although usually too retiring to be a leader in social reforms, gave much attention in her later writings to such reforms. Socially, the family had always been connected primarily with New York and only secondarily with Boston; Miss Sedgwick made it quite clear in her later writings that Boston (and the world of Boston's causes) was where she really belonged—the realm later described by Henry James in *The Bostonians*.

Unfortunately, Miss Sedgwick's social treatises are quite

dated now not only because they are concerned with social injustices which no longer exist but also because these injustices could never have been corrected by the answers she provided. Moreover, she never intended her social treatises, notably her didactic tales, to have the literary merits of *Hope Leslie* and *Redwood*. These social treatises were intended to have only an immediate and not a lasting value; they were intended to provide solutions for social injustices which existed in Miss Sedgwick's America. While these writings received little attention from literary critics, they received much attention from critics of American society. One of these critics dismissed novels because they "originate no virtuous feeling—they lead to no self-examination, no conviction of one's own worthlessness." On the other hand, he believed that Miss Sedgwick's didactic tale *The Poor Rich Man and the Rich Poor Man* might well "inculcate the true principles by which the goods of this life are to be estimated, and our conduct regulated. . . ."

This reviewer, like others who favorably noticed her didactic tales, ignored entirely questions of the book's literary merit—or lack of it. He was solely concerned with its *didactic* moral quality. "We would, if we could," he concluded, "send [this book] to every fireside in our land—of the rich as well as the poor—though to the last we especially recommend it. To the publication of such books we would ever lend our utmost aid, convinced that above all others they conduce to the real good of the community; and in conclusion, we may express the hope that the fair author has but given an earnest of what she intends to do in a line of writing that has been too much neglected in this country, and which is of paramount importance at the present time."[5]

Miss Sedgwick's later reviewers and readers—including William Ellery Channing and Ralph Waldo Emerson—seem to have been less concerned about whether her social treatises were good literature than about whether her "causes" were the right ones. Jacksonians found particular reason to praise her later works, for most of the didactic tales encouraged the common man to improve his lot in the world. As a good Unitarian, Miss Sedgwick believed that all men are inherently good and that, if they will make use of those talents which God has given them, they will ultimately be happy and successful in their lives. The only major difference between social classes, she believed, was manners; and the teaching of good manners became a central objective of her fiction. She seems to have believed that, when all classes could express themselves through the same forms of behavior, democracy would be at last a reality.

II *The Morals of Manners*

In January, 1834, Miss Sedgwick received a letter from the Reverend Henry Ware which outlined a plan for "a series of narratives, between a formal tale and a common tract," to illustrate "the practical character and influences of Christianity."[6] He asked her to write one of the volumes, and she complied with *Home* (1835) which was dedicated to "Farmers and Mechanics." It was a phenomenal success and in six years went through no less than fifteen editions.

This success encouraged Miss Sedgwick to write more of the same, dedicated to such people as "My Young Countrywomen—the Future Ministers of the Charities of the Home," and dealing with such themes as "the failures of one party in the contract between employers and employed," a subject she found "momentous."[7] The theme is indeed a momentous one, but Miss Sedgwick, who, in general, seems to have believed that a little Christian charity could solve nearly all problems, was somewhat ignorant of social realities. *The Poor Rich Man and the Rich Poor Man* (1836) went through sixteen editions in less than three years. And in less than two years, the third of her didactic tales, *Live and Let Live: or, Domestic Service Illustrated,* (1837) went through no less than twelve editions. Whatever our opinions of her social theories may be, it is clear that many of her contemporaries found what she had to say worth reading.

In a less perceptive moment, William Ellery Channing claimed that this didactic trilogy formed "an era in our literature," and he said of the third volume that "thousands will be the better and happier for it."[8] Having read *The Poor Rich Man,* one eminent divine, the Boston Unitarian minister Dr. Joseph Tuckerman, wrote to Miss Sedgwick that "most gratefully do I rejoice that this power is consecrated by you to the highest and noblest ends."[9] Joseph Curtis, a noted educator whose biography Miss Sedgwick later wrote, added that, "in all his experience, he had never witnessed so much good fruit from the publication of any book."[10] Bryant recorded that one publisher, while correcting proofs for one of the books, "was fairly carried away by his emotions, and could not restrain himself from weeping profusely."[11]

Ralph Waldo Emerson liked Miss Sedgwick's idealized characterizations, and Orestes Brownson had some kind things to say about another of her didactic volumes, *Means and Ends,* in *The Boston Quarterly Review.* After indicating that the author "aims well, and the tendency of her writings is in the right direction," he noted, however, that "Sedgwick is not truly democratic; she does not seem to have fully comprehended the real evil of existing society, and does not perceive that the remedies she proposes, can at best but partially mitigate it."[12] Brownson was correct; Miss Sedgwick never considered herself the social equal of those in the lower classes; she was never "truly democratic." Although she later wrote that the "rustic duties" performed by her brothers as children were good because these chores cultivated "sympathies with the laboring classes," her views were tainted by her father's Federalism which taught her that her good breeding made her socially superior to many Americans.[13]

III *Home, Sweet Home*

Apparently few readers were disconcerted by Miss Sedgwick's aristocratic attitude; most seem to have been content to say with the English writer Harriet Martineau that the didactic tales were "wonderfully beautiful."[14] To this comment Miss Martineau added that the books "present pictures of the household life of New England which [Miss Sedgwick] knows so well, and loves so dearly."[15] In this respect, Miss Martineau stated one of the major reasons for the success of the later tales: their local color. They offer very general descriptions of New England scenery and make use of New England manners and social customs. For example, a city dweller in *Live and Let Live* is "increasing her value by learning to perform domestic offices well."[16] Just as if she were a New England country housewife, she has "learned in her novitiate the most thorough mode of dusting, how most accurately to make a bed, the best way of cleaning plate, and that heavy duty of our winters, polishing brasses."[17] (At this point one might well reflect on Miss Sedgwick's interest in education for women.)

In mid-nineteenth century America, domestics could be hired at very low wages. Presumably it was not necessary for a lady of the time to learn even the rudiments of house cleaning, but Miss Sedgwick's heroines who employ domestics can also clean house as well as any woman from a New England farm. In an age in which cities were becoming increasingly important, the Sedgwick tales served a function similar to that of Currier and Ives prints: the didactic tales were reminders of the country life which could still be found in the environs of the great cities but which would inevitably be replaced by growing industrial and financial centers and by a more sophisticated pattern of life. The sons of country families— men like Cornelius Vanderbilt, Daniel Drew, Phineas T. Barnum, like Bryant, Horace Greeley, and Fitz-Greene Halleck—were leaving for New York; and Miss Sedgwick's book provided the reassurance that, even if these men found money and fame in the city, it was in the country that good manners and morals thrived best.

Not surprisingly, the heroes and heroines of Miss Sedgwick's didactic tales always yearn for country life when they, for some reason, are forced to live in the city. In the harshest winter months, when Stockbridge was isolated from the world, Miss Sedgwick lived in New York where she met many who shared her literary interests; but, like her heroes and heroines, she preferred country life; and, with the coming of spring, she always returned to the

Berkshires. Furthermore, while she was in New York, she always lived in the homes of her relatives—never in the homes of her friends. In short, she maintained in New York a strong family domestic life much like that which she found in the country.

To see Miss Sedgwick's idealization of New England domesticity most clearly, it is best to concentrate on the first of her didactic tales, *Home,* which is in part based on her own family life as a child. The town of Greenbrook, where the story opens and closes, is clearly based on Stockbridge, the small village surrounded by a pastoral landscape; but Miss Sedgwick says that Greenbrook might be located in any state in New England; for in this area "there is such a unity of character and similarity of condition, that what is true of one [state] may be probable of all." However, Miss Sedgwick then describes the stream from which Greenbrook takes its name by quoting some lines from Bryant's poem "Green River," and the original Green River of which Bryant wrote is located near the Sedgwick family home in Stockbridge.[18]

The plot of the tale can be quickly summarized. William Barclay is a native of the country, but his work as a printer requires him to live in the city—much as the Sedgwicks were forced to spend some of their childhood in New York, Philadelphia, and Boston because their father's political and legal careers required his presence in these cities. Barclay and his wife much prefer to live in the country; but, since it is necessary for them to remain in New York, they decide that, nonetheless, they will do their best to give their children a training in all the manners and morals characteristic of Christian New Englanders. The substance of the book involves brief pictures of the Barclays' family life and shows the parents' successful attempts to instill these manners and morals in their children. Toward the end of the tale, the Barclays realize their wish to return to Greenbrook and to operate the family farm. Although circumstances have made it necessary for them to live in the city, they have managed to preserve their ideal New England characteristics.

In *Home,* Miss Sedgwick clearly spells out what these

ideal New England manners and morals are. To begin, William Barclay is described as a man "capable, diligent, frugal, and willing to dispense with the superfluities."[19] To him, home "is a word, that . . . expresses every motive and aid to virtue."[20] Since the author believed so strongly in domestic life, it should not surprise us to learn that her hero believes "that a household, governed in obedience to the Christian social law, would present as perfect an image of heaven, as the infirmity of human nature, and the imperfections in the constitution of human affairs, would permit."[21]

For democracy to succeed fully, Miss Sedgwick concludes, education should be the product of living at home. Indeed, "the *sine quâ non* of a New-England mother" is "a good education for her son."[22] According to Mr. Barclay, "the equality, which is the basis of our institutions, should also, as far as possible, be the basis of education."[23] And, as he has proved, equality can be taught in the home; "I have labored to convince my boys, that there is nothing vulgar in the mechanic professions,—no particular reasons for envying the lawyer and the doctor."[24] The main difference between classes, as Miss Sedgwick sees it, lies not in riches but in manners. Mr. Barclay, for example, dreams of an ideal "working man," "whose general attainments and *manners* qualify him for polished society"—which means that he "has some acquaintance with science, draws beautifully, and writes graceful verses."[25] When we are all mannerly, we will be equal; but, needless to add, there are practical things more important than mere accomplishments. One girl knows that "it is worth a great deal more to know how to sweep, than how to dance."[26] Indeed, the most common domestic activities can teach more manners than the greatest social functions; a well-ordered meal teaches "punctuality, order, neatness, temperance, self-denial, kindness, generosity, and hospitality."[27] Such manners of the home like those of the table must be learned if America is to be a full democracy; for, "there is nothing," as Mr. Barclay says in *Home*, "that tends more to the separation into classes than difference of manners."[28] Barclay, a true Christian, even undertakes to instruct the immigrant Irish in the necessities of good manners as his own contribution toward the day when "farmers and mechanics are to range with the highest in the land."[29]

The best manners, the best social institutions, are, of course, practiced in the country—in this case, Greenbrook, the Barclay family's "Jerusalem, to which the heart made all its pilgrimages."[30] The sons of New England families may be leaving their homes to find fortunes in the cities, but they are taking with them their memories of good homes and good manners. "The Yankee boy, from the earliest period of forecast, dreams of seeking his fortune in the richer soil and kinder climate which his far-spread country provides for him"—in this case, the West. "He goes, but his heart lingers at the *homestead*."[31] He brings with him the best feature of the New England small town, the democratic center where "the intrinsic claims of each individual are known and admitted."[32] In a place like Greenbrook, "whether a man be lawyer, farmer, or mechanic, matters not, if he be intelligent and respectable"— and the emphasis is upon "respectable."[33] New England triumphs: its manners and morals suggest a way through which democracy can become a full reality in this country; and as New Englanders emigrate westward, they will bring this democratic way of life with them. The regional customs have now been given a national significance.

After *Home* was published, Miss Sedgwick's brother Theodore published the first volume of his *Public and Private Economy*. Ten years before, he had written that, in Europe, "a man is worth but little more than any other animal"; but, in America, "an honest laborious man . . . is buried with as much respect as any in the land."[34] That "honest laborious man" became the hero of Theodore's *Public and Private Economy*, an attempt to promote the type of life represented by a merchant in a small, New England town. Forgetting the days when the Sedgwick brothers and sisters had found that Stockbridge provided little excitement, Miss Sedgwick and Theodore idealized the rural lives they had experienced as children. Theodore's medium was the treatise on economics; Miss Sedgwick's was, of course, the didactic tale.

Another example of Miss Sedgwick's sentimental accounts of New England country life is *The Boy of Mount Rhigi* (1848). Set in an area not far from Stockbridge, the book offers some pleasant, albeit nostalgic, descriptions of the Western Massachusetts and Connecticut countrysides. The story involves two natives of this region, the boyhood friends, Clapham Dunn and Harry Davis. The former is reared by parents who have little concern for his moral character, but the latter's mother carefully educates her son as a Christian. Miss Sedgwick was somewhat less interested in providing local color than in awakening, "in those of our young people who have been carefully nurtured, a sense of their duty to those who are less favored."[35] Harry is able to save his friend from an immoral life by passing on to him the moral characteristics acquired at home. There is little here that does not contribute to Miss Sedgwick's didactic purpose. "It is with wet eyes," one minister told the author, "that I hasten to thank you for this charming work, as full of wisdom as of genius, of love as truth, of piety as pure and solid morality."[36]

Despite its superficiality and its sentimental morality, there is, nonetheless, something attractive in the sincerity of Miss Sedgwick's didacticism. Although Miss Sedgwick's solutions for social problems seem hopelessly inadequate today, she was basing her assertions on what she had come to consider a thoroughly happy childhood—one in which strictly obeyed codes of manners and morals guaranteed a contented domestic life. The fact that her childhood had not been altogether as happy as she later thought does not make her fictional pictures of that earlier Stockbridge and its "sacred mansion" any less charming.

In an era of causes and moral literary instruction, Miss Sedgwick certainly fit the classification of "blue-stocking"—that is, in a somewhat pedantic fashion, she suggested in her writings solutions for what she considered the major faults of American society. In fact, she knew little of politics or economics, and her knowledge of lower-class life was derived almost entirely from rumor. As a member of committees formed to achieve social reforms, she visited such institutions as prisons and workhouses;

but, unlike Charles Dickens, for example, she never personally experienced lower-class life. Her brothers undoubtedly provided her with some knowledge of economics and politics; and yet, in her didactic tales, it seems
as if the only major problems in American society are those
which involve poor manners and weak home lives. Correct
these faults, Miss Sedgwick seems to say, and happiness
will prevail. Clearly there were many readers who were
willing to listen to her, for her trilogy—*Home, The Poor
Rich Man,* and *Live and Let Live*—became, as *Harper's*
remarked at the time of her death, "one of the most popular series of works ever published."[37] There was, however,
at least one American who found Miss Sedgwick's solutions
insufficient. As one critic has pointed out, Herman Melville
probably was thinking of such volumes as *The Poor Rich
Man and the Rich Poor Man* when he wrote "Poor Man's
Pudding and Rich Man's Crumbs."[38] "Of all the prepos-
terous assumptions of humanity over humanity," Melville
wrote, "nothing exceeds most of the criticisms made on
the habits of the poor by the well-housed, well-warmed,
and well-fed."[39]

Miss Sedgwick's didactic tales belong in a class with
such mid-nineteenth century best-sellers as T. S. Arthur's
Ten Nights in a Barroom (1854), William Hallock's *The
Mountain Miller* (1838), and Harriet Beecher Stowe's
Uncle Tom's Cabin (1851–52). Each of these books
attempted to correct some social fault: intemperance,
religious infidelity, and slavery, respectively. Miss Sedgwick's books, likewise, attempted to correct a social fault—
in this case, the abyss which she believed a difference in
manners had created between social classes. She encouraged
her readers to act like her ideal New Englanders—charitable,
kind, unpretentious, and hard working—people very much
like the Sedgwicks themselves.

Miss Sedgwick's instructions in manners served a
function in a nation bordered to the west by a raw frontier. Her books were as valuable to Western settlers as
they were to immigrants: for both groups, her books were
guides to the cultivation of manners. There were more than
a hundred etiquette books published between 1830 and

1860—indeed, James D. Hart once called this "the age of the etiquette book"—and surely Miss Sedgwick's didactic tales served the same function as these manuals. In addition, her books provided an entertaining narrative, thereby making the acquisition of manners a pleasant enterprise.

Besides *The Boy of Mount Rhigi* and the trilogy which began with *Home,* Miss Sedgwick wrote a number of children's works of relatively negligible significance. *Means and Ends* (1839), written "for girls from ten to sixteen years of age," sought to convince its audience that education was extremely important for young girls— but Miss Sedgwick's ideal female education was one which gave much emphasis to the best ways of washing dishes and cleaning house.[40]

Other minor children's works included *The Morals of Manners* (1846) and *Facts and Fancies for School Day Reading* (1848), both of which are essentially etiquette books. Miss Sedgwick had acquired a substantial reputation as a story-teller for children—all her stories having, of course, a specific moral to teach. *A Love-token for Children* (1838) was a collection of some of these stories, and no doubt many parents were pleased with this book as a present for birthdays. On the other hand, it is worth asking if all children were equally moved and instructed by Miss Sedgwick's didacticism and by the frequent sentimentality found in these writings. Did children in fact respond sympathetically to such sentiments as this: "the still, small voice of their prayer arose, and God was there."[41] Perhaps children were interested in Miss Sedgwick's sentimentality and her religious overtones; and they may have learned much from her didacticism; but within a decade of her death, Mark Twain's *The Adventures of Tom Sawyer* (1876) approached the field of children's literature with somewhat less didacticism, sentimentality, and piety. *Tom Sawyer,* not *The Morals of Manners,* proved to be the kind of book which the new generation of children preferred to read; consequently, Miss Sedgwick's didactic works for children were soon out of print.

Miss Sedgwick once called one author's writings, "sweet-

ened slops and water-gruels that impair the mental digestion"—a criticism which an ungenerous twentieth-century
reader might make of Miss Sedgwick's children's books.[42]
Indeed, there seems to have been at least one nineteenth-
century reader whose "mental digestion" was rather "im-
paired" by these works—a New Yorker who, finding a reference to marbles in one of the tales, begged her to change
it to a game of kite, because, he said, "marbles were immoral."[43]

IV *Literary Excercises*

During the years Miss Sedgwick was writing her didactic
tales, she was also contributing to magazines and annuals.
Most of these pieces involve domestic life or the small
town, American history or the beauties and pleasures of
the countryside. There are even such stories as "The Irish
Girl," which repeats the plea in *Home* for a greater understanding between Americans and immigrants. Throughout
almost all these works, there is the feeling that life
was never better than in the America of the second
quarter of the nineteenth century—especially as witnessed
in Stockbridge and Lenox, Massachusetts.

Miss Sedgwick made two collections of *Tales and
Sketches* (1835 and 1844), as well as several collections
of short works intended primarily for children; but even
these collected pieces, presumably those which she considered her best, are not especially interesting. Almost
all are obvious reworkings, at a minor level, of ideas she
had treated in her novels and didactic tales. There were
many annuals and magazines which published shorter
works by Miss Sedgwick, and many of these works were
never collected or republished. As Miss Sedgwick herself must have realized, they would not have been worth
the costs of reprinting.

Miss Sedgwick also wrote a biography, *Lucretia Maria
Davidson*, for Jared Sparks' *Library of American Biography*. Miss Davidson was a consumptive young Romantic
poet whose work attracted favorable attention from Edgar
Allen Poe. Like her sister Margaret, Lucretia Davidson

used such topics as floral arrangements, sickness, and death in her poetry. Appropriately for people who spent so much time writing about melancholy subjects, both sisters died young. Shortly after Lucretia Davidson's death, Miss Sedgwick was commissioned to write her biography. (Washington Irving wrote the biography of Margaret, who, incidentally, had once composed twenty-three verses about a rose that Miss Sedgwick gave her.)

Lucretia, who was only nine when she burst upon the literary scene with "On the Death of My Robin," spent her remaining seven years producing more than a hundred poems considered worthy of publication—including "On seeing, at a Concert, the public performance of a Female Dwarf." Another verse, "On the Death of Queen Caroline," begins, "Star of England! Brunswick's pride! / Thou hast suffer'd, droop'd, and died!"[44] Poetry of this sort, which Mark Twain parodied in *The Adventures of Huckleberry Finn,* found a large audience in pre-Civil War America; and enough readers were interested in Lucretia Davidson's life to insure numerous reprintings of the biography.

The biography was published in 1839, the same year that Miss Sedgwick entered upon still another literary adventure; a two-volume commentary on Europe, finally published in 1841. This book could have been her most interesting for readers today, for the contact between the New England author and Europe could have resulted in a detailed analysis of the differences between the manners and customs of the Old World and the New. Unfortunately, *Letters from Abroad to Kindred at Home* contains no really satisfying account of what it was like for an American of the time to visit countries so extraordinarily different from the new nation. The Puritan in her did rise at times, however, as when she went to the ballet to see Marie Taglioni: "there is music in every movement of her arms; and if she would restrict herself within the limits of decency, there could not be a more exquisite spectacle of its kind than her dancing." The objection was severe: "could not this grace be equally demonstrated with a skirt a few inches longer and rather less transparent?"[45] To a true democrat, English royalty was also disappointing. Having seen Queen Victoria at the opera, Miss Sedgwick wrote that "she is a plain little body enough, as we saw when she protruded her head to bow to the high people in the box next to her. . . . Ordinary is the word for her."[46]

Miss Sedgwick was too much in love with her Berkshires to be an adequate observer of British and European civilizations. Even the best English scenery could never compare with her native landscape: "If an Englishman were to select a single view in his country to give a stranger the best idea of the characteristics of English rural scenery, it would probably be that of Richmond Hill. . . . And yet, shall I confess it to you, I would have given all the pleasure I should get from it for a life-time for one glance from S[tockbridge]'s hill at the valley with its wooden houses, straggling brown fences, and ragged husbandry!"[47]

All three comments—on the ballet, the Queen, and the English landscape—were made shortly after Miss Sedgwick arrived in Britain. Already she had decided that anything on the other side of the Atlantic could never equal anything in America and she gave Europe just about as much chance to prove itself as Edmund Stuart had given America in *Clarence*. And *Letters from Abroad* was offensive to anyone living in the countries about which Miss Sedgwick was not appreciative. The volumes were attacked by *The Athanaeum* as "idle prying and mistaken."[48] And the very English Henry Fothergill Chorley noted that

Miss Sedgwick has been returning the compliment of all English journalists, by putting us all round on paper, to a degree which is too bad. She asked, it seems, poor dear Miss Mitford's servants what wages they received, and the like; and, I hear, has written that which is likely most sadly to compromise some of the Italian refugees in America, who were negotiating, with the Austrian Government, for a restoration to their families. I liked her so well in private, as an honest-minded, simple-mannered, cultivated woman, that I am really more vexed than there is any occasion for.[49]

Americans were not bothered by the book's inadequacies, however, and *Letters from Abroad to Kindred at Home* was enthusiastically welcomed. According to *The Christian Review*, Miss Sedgwick's account was related "with all the gushing sympathy befitting each relation and circumstance which passed before her."[50]

V *Married or Single?*

"Miss Sedgwick," wrote Margaret Fuller, "though she inclines to the private path, and wishes that, by the cultivation of character, might should vindicate right, sets limits nowhere, and her objects and inducements are pure. They are the free and careful cultivation of the powers that have been given, with an aim at moral and intellectual perfection."[51] Miss Sedgwick's desire that, through "the cultivation of character, might should vindicate right" is, of course, central to her fiction. An idealist, furthermore, she did not wish simply to improve the general condition of society; she wished to perfect it; and, consequently, her didactic fiction provided readers with ideal examples to be imitated.

In her last two works, *Married or Single?* (1857) and *Memoir of Joseph Curtis, a Model Man* (1858), Miss Sedgwick provided ideal models such as she had provided in her didactic tales. *Married or Single?* was written to disprove the popular belief "that a woman's single life must be useless or undignified—that she is but an adjunct of man—in her best state a helm merely to guide the nobler vessel."[52] Miss Sedgwick's ideal single woman is Grace Herbert, a member of a socially élite and wealthy New York family and a woman of impeccable manners and morals. She is engaged to marry a man named Horace Copley, who proves to be unworthy of her. Grace then decides to make her way in the world without the aid of a husband—a decision that was quite unusual in pre-Civil War America when a woman's place was, of course, literally in the home.

However, Miss Sedgwick does not allow her heroine to pursue an independent course for long; she soon falls in love with Archibald Lisle, the hero of the book and Grace's equal in morals and manners. The book ends not with a picture of her single life but with her marriage. She has bowed to what Miss Sedgwick calls "the great law of Nature, by which, in every province of her infinitely various kingdom, all 'kindred drops are melted into one.' "[53] Grace's decision to remain single, as Miss Sedgwick makes clear in her preface, must not be treated scornfully, but marriage, "the great law of Nature," provides the better life for a woman, when, of course, there is the ideal man, an Archibald Lisle, available. The conclusion of *Married or Single?*—namely that, for a woman, married life may well be preferable to single life—is predictable on the basis of Miss Sedgwick's earlier writings and her biography. *Married or Single?*, Miss Sedgwick's last novel, appropriately concludes with the same faith in marriage and domestic life that is to be found throughout her works and her biography.

Married or Single? received little attention from critics or the public. For one thing, this book was her first major effort in nine years—the first since the publication of *The Boy of Mount Rhigi*—and most of her original public was either dead or more interested in such novelists as Harriet Beecher Stowe and Maria Cummins, whose reputations dated from the early 1850's. Among Miss Sedgwick's contemporaries, Cooper had been dead seven years; Irving had retired to his home on the Hudson to complete his biography of George Washington; and only Bryant remained active in the social and literary life of New York, but he was now known less as a poet than as the crusading editor of the New York *Evening Post.* A new generation of writers interested the public and the critics; and Miss Sedgwick found herself—as indeed she had expected—with a far less enthusiastic audience than that which had greeted her earlier works.[54] The journals either did not review the novel or gave it little attention.

The lack of critical and popular attention was justified as well as expected, for *Married or Single?* contains some of Miss Sedgwick's least inspired writing—pages of dialogue which too often restate her contentions but offer little or no characterization. According to Sister Mary Michael Welsh's *Catharine Maria Sedgwick*, Miss Sedgwick's idealization of Grace Herbert and Archibald Lisle "has resulted in rendering both rather vapid"—a fair conclusion, although it might be added that the novel's didactic purpose required this idealization of characters.[55] There are, however, occasional delightful passages in which Miss Sedgwick satirizes the New York aristocracy of wealth as she had done in *Clarence*—indeed, a minor figure named Mrs. Seton in *Married or Single?* may have been patterned after Mrs. A. T. Stewart, a woman who rose to the top of New York society with the aid of an immense fortune accumulated by her husband in the dry goods business. The Seton mansion, "like many other piles of brick and mortar belonging to our 'merchant princes' . . . , almost equaled the palaces of Europe in the luxury of space, and outrivaled them in costly furniture, and abounding decorations of bronzes, scores of statuettes, with some sculpture from the modern statuaries, and beautiful pictures—not *all* copies."[56]

Miss Sedgwick's evident knowledge of the habits and customs of upper-class New Yorkers during the mid-nineteenth century makes the reader wish that she had employed her talents in sketching that aristocratic life as fully as Edith Wharton was to do a half-century later in *The Custom of the Country, The Age of Innocence*, and other novels. Unfortunately, Miss Sedgwick's satire of the New York aristocracy of wealth is limited to a few brief passages; she was clearly more interested in her ideal hero and heroine.

In 1858, Miss Sedgwick published her final work, the *Memoir of Joseph Curtis, a Model Man*. In it, as in *Married or Single?*, she provided an ideal figure to be emulated by young readers, particularly boys. The book, as its subtitle indicates, provided the portrait of "a Model Man." Joseph Curtis was offered as an ideal for boys to emulate just as Grace Herbert was intended as an ideal for girls. Curtis had been one of Miss Sedgwick's friends. Both an educator and an eminently charitable man, he spent his life among the poor of New York and worked to educate them and to improve their lives materially. The book is extraordinarily didactic, and good characteristics are underscored. Hardly a fault is pointed out, although Miss Sedgwick notes that, regrettably, Curtis chewed tobacco—a major sin, apparently, for ". . all his life [he] bitterly lamented its mastery over him."[57] Bryant—who apparently never read *Married or Single?* —was among those who had many good things to say about the *Memoir*.[58] He considered the book a worthy monument to a distinguished man.

Miss Sedgwick published no books during the last nine years of her life, although her earlier novels and some of the didactic tales, including *Home* and *Live and Let Live*, remained in print; indeed, four years after her death, Harper and Brothers was still selling twelve of her works. Furthermore, when the early history of American literature was discussed, she was still grouped with Cooper, Bryant, and Irving as one of the founders of literature in this country. However, with the increasing importance of Harriet Beecher Stowe, Maria Cummins, and other, younger novelists who shared a large popularity, the attention given to Miss Sedgwick's works continued to decline. Mrs. Stowe, who was among Miss Sedgwick's circle, employed New England color more fully than the author of *Redwood* had. Whereas Miss Sedgwick was capable—as in *Redwood*—of sketching out a handful of New England characters, Mrs. Stowe—in *The Minister's Wooing* (1859), *The Pearl of Orr's Island* (1862), and other books—recreated entire New England communities. *The Pearl of Orr's Island* gave readers a full sense of a Maine settlement, and *The Minister's Wooing* recreated the Newport, Rhode Island, of the late eighteenth century. Miss Sedgwick in such books as *A New-England Tale*, *Redwood*, and *Home* portrayed the life of the New England family. Mrs. Stowe also portrayed this family life but went on to give a larger picture of New England communities.

Maria Cummins, on the other hand, in *The Lamplighter* (1854) gave a fuller picture of lower-class life in the cities than Miss Sedgwick had done in any of her novels. Furthermore, Miss Cummins proved herself Miss Sedgwick's equal in describing the habits of the upper class; *The Lamplighter* contains extensive descriptions of fashionable life in the city and at mid-nineteenth-century resorts. In short, Miss Cummins, who had been a student at Elizabeth Sedgwick's school in Lenox, was able to provide readers with more extensive accounts of both lower-class and aristocratic life than were to be found in *Clarence, Home,* or *Married or Single?* Nor, finally, was the younger novelist's purpose any less didactic than Miss Sedgwick's; and parents could be assured that their children would receive much moral instruction from the novels of Maria Cummins.

Mrs. Stowe and Miss Cummins were able to do what Miss Sedgwick had always done in her writings—but, quite simply, they did more of it, and in the 1850's and 1860's their books were enormously popular. *The Lamplighter,* for example, is believed to have sold twenty thousand copies within the first twenty days after its publication.[59] Although the sales figures for *Married or Single?* have not survived, there is nothing in Miss Sedgwick's letters or the reviews of the book to suggest that it ever attracted much popular attention. Miss Sedgwick had become a writer respected primarily, it seems, for her place in the history of American literature.

VI *Final Years*

Married or Single? was published a year after the death of Miss Sedgwick's brother Charles; and, by 1857, Miss Sedgwick was the only surviving member of her immediate family. Shortly after the third and final volume of Theodore Sedgwick's *Public and Private Economy* appeared, he gave a lecture to the members of the Democratic Party in the nearby city of Pittsfield. As he was leaving the platform, he suffered a stroke and died shortly after, November 7, 1839. Less than two years later, Robert, who had spent most of his life as a New York lawyer, was dead; and Charles died in 1856. "God only knows how I have loved my brothers," Miss Sedgwick had written to William Ellery Channing at the time of Robert's death, "the union of feeling, of taste, of principle, of affection I have had with them. No closer tie has ever weakened that which began with my being. I have no recollection beyond the time when they made my happiness."[60]

Shortly after the death of Charles, Miss Sedgwick wrote from the Lenox home that she could not leave the place at that time. "Here," she said,

only the vacant places answer to the cries of my spirit; here the form has not departed. I see my brother on the sofa—on the piazza. I spread his table for him. I start at the sound of his voice. I go down into the garden, and look at the "corn," and the "Lima beans," and the "tomatoes," and tell him how they are growing. He still sits at my chamber window; his light, as well as his shadow, is every where; and while the summer lasts, the season that bears his visible impress, I can not go away.[61]

At the time, she was at work on the manuscript of *Married or Single?* Considering the large amount of family love evident in the tribute to the memory of her brother, it should not surprise us to discover the reaffirmation of domesticity and marriage in her final work of fiction.

Her brother Henry's wife died in 1859. Robert's wife died three years later. The same year, Elizabeth Sedgwick, Charles' wife, closed the doors of her Lenox school for the last time. Until her death three years later, she and Miss Sedgwick remained close friends. Theodore's wife, Susan, died in January, 1867, six months before Miss Sedgwick; and most of Miss Sedgwick's friends also died during her later years. Poor health kept her from visiting those who had survived, including the most famous of her literary friends, William Cullen Bryant. She spent most of her last years at the home of a niece outside Boston. "I have a balcony out of Kate's window in the pine wood, where I lie all day," she wrote toward the end of her life, "and where the mercies and love of God are continually pressing upon my senses. But 'tis hard work . . . to be sick, and helpless, and useless!"[62] This passage was written on July 19, 1867, and less than two weeks later, July 31, she was dead. She was buried beneath a small cross between the graves of "Mumbet" and her brother Charles in the Sedgwick section of the cemetery in Stockbridge.

VII Life and Letters

It is unfortunate that no record survives of the visit between Miss Sedgwick and John Greenleaf Whittier, for there is something especially fitting in the meeting between the Quaker poet and the older novelist—both of whom maintained a belief in the perfectibility of man and both of whom were, like their fellow New Englanders William Ellery Channing and Ralph Waldo Emerson, idealists who believed that America would soon correct its social injustices and narrow the gap between social classes. Their meeting took place shortly before Miss Sedgwick's death; and, a generation later, the founding of the great American fortunes and the reorganization of American business by Andrew Carnegie, John D. Rockefeller, and others had created an America wholly foreign to the somewhat simpler world of Miss Sedgwick's childhood in Stockbridge and Whittier's in the farming countryside of rural Massachusetts.

Ten years after Sarah Orne Jewett published *The Country of the Pointed Firs* (1896), she read Miss Sedgwick's *Life and Letters* in the company of a friend and discovered an earlier, simpler world:

We each passed it to the other to read some delightful page, and "the other" would read on in silence until a craving for sympathy made her selfish enough to pass it back again. I did not know how good it was. I fancied it had been written in the dull times of "Memoirs," but I was quite wrong; it was just as well to wait and grow a good deal older before I went back to it, and Mrs. Cabot had not opened it for many years. It is a charming picture of my mother's and your grand-mother's New England. Mrs. Kemble's letter at the end is one to learn by heart. There is a page, too, about the advantages of country life, that made me "fire up" about Berwick as I used in my best days.[63]

At the turn of the century when Miss Jewett wrote this statement she was recognized as the greatest of the New England local-color writers; and, like Miss Sedgwick and other earlier New England writers, she found in country villages people who are as moral and humane as the best bred of the city's aristocrats. Although no documentary evidence has yet been found to show that Miss Jewett's writings were directly influenced by Miss Sedgwick's, *The Country of the Pointed Firs* was as much a record of New England pastoral life as *Redwood* had been when it was published more than seventy years before.

Miss Sedgwick died when New England was about to lose much of its influence in national affairs. There were no more Daniel Websters to influence American politics and no more Emersons to influence American literature. The nation's economic center was New York, not Boston. There were fewer people moving to New England—as the Barclays do in *Home*—than there were New Englanders moving to New York or the Midwest. Miss Sedgwick wrote of a New England which was still a major force in the developing nation—a New England which largely disappeared soon after her death. In the obituary of Miss Sedgwick published in *Harper's Monthly Magazine*, a sense of her New England is captured in a description of Stockbridge:

Stockbridge is a long, broad, grassy, silent elm-embowered street, with a range of pleasant houses upon either side, standing separately, each retired in its lovely seclusion of foliage. The cliffs of Monument Mountain rise beyond the Housatonic, a placid little stream that loiters through the meadows. And so profound is the repose of the whole scene, so free even from the murmur of mill-wheels, that the stranger looks curiously to see if there is so much as a shop in the village; and as he climbs the hill towards Lenox, and looks down upon the romantic valley, he bears away only the soft image of pastoral peace.[64]

CHAPTER 7

The Reputation

Ever since [Miss Sedgwick's] entrance into the world of letters her literary productions have been mainly, in every sense of the word, American. Not only have the scenes and incidents of her works of fiction been drawn from the history of this country or its domestic manners, but her more directly useful and perhaps most praiseworthy efforts have all been an illustration of its social habits and tendencies. *Besides this, there are perhaps none of our writers, whose works in their spirit or style more completely reflect the more prominent characteristics of the American mind.* They are marked less by the refinements of highly cultivated taste and imagination than by a rigorous straightforwardness of purpose and practical energy, of which the principal ingredient is that rare quality in authorship, good common sense.

—*The Literary World*; October 6, 1849.[1]

DURING the nineteenth century, considerable attention was given to Miss Sedgwick's works by the public and by critics, as well as by her contemporary writers—Bryant, Cooper, Irving, Poe, Emerson, Melville, Hawthorne, and others. Of these writers, as we have seen, only Melville offered harsh criticism; indeed, Hawthorne concluded that she was "our most truthful novelist."[2] In order to assess Miss Sedgwick's achievement, it is helpful to re-examine the major reasons she was so widely praised in her lifetime. The first of the reasons is of purely historical interest: she was among the first of the internationally known American writers. As late as 1871, a critic in *Harper's New Monthly Magazine* included her with Irving as one of "those who first created an American literature worthy [of] the name"; and both Poe and George William Curtis drew attention to the fact that she was once the most famous woman writer in America—a precedence which "was never seriously threatened," Curtis added, until Mrs. Stowe's *Uncle Tom's Cabin* was published in 1851–52.[3]

Furthermore, as Bryant wrote, "her works were admired, and added to our household libraries without asking, as had too often been the case in regard to other American authors, permission from the critics of Great Britain."[4] Miss Sedgwick's fame—which soon spread throughout England and the Continent—had its origins at home. "Perhaps she is the single exception to the remark with which we have commenced these papers," wrote a contributor to the British *Athenaeum*, "the one native writer to whom Americans have done justice, unprompted by foreign criticism. Her novels are extremely popular in the United States."[5]

One of the major reasons that Miss Sedgwick's novels attracted favorable attention in the United States was her use of native American materials in her fiction—a fact which *The Literary World* drew to the attention of its readers. "The scenes" in her novels, wrote the commentator for *The Athenaeum*, "are laid in the country in which she lives; and the scenery is described, and the manners of the people delineated with masterly truth and power."[6] Although Miss Sedgwick was interested in all things related to American life, much of her fiction centered on New England. The history, religion, scenery, manners, and customs of this region provided her with materials for her best-known novels, *Redwood* and *Hope Leslie.* The Becket storekeeper in *A New-England Tale* is the first Yankee peddler in American fiction; and among Miss Sedgwick's most successful characters is Deborah Lenox, the Yankee spinster who acts as Miss Sedgwick's moral commentator in *Redwood.* Furthermore, her idealized version of New England family life is found in her description of the Lenoxes in *Redwood,* the Lees in *The Linwoods,* the Barclays in *Home,* and so forth.

Miss Sedgwick's concern with American materials—scenery, manners, history, and so forth—was to be expected from one as enthusiastic about the American experiment in democracy as she was. One summer evening in 1843, she listened as Cooper argued "that his own country was below France, Italy, and even England in civilization, intellectual development, *morals*, and manners; that we were going in every thing backward; that in common honesty we were below any other nation."[7] The tirade amused Miss Sedgwick; "he is," she remarked about Cooper, "a perfect John Bull in shape, dimensions, action, even to the growl."[8] Miss Sedgwick shared with her country-men a Romantic vision of the American future and its "Manifest Destiny." She described the lands stretching back from the banks of the Mississippi River as "the pre-serves of the Lord of earth's manor for his children"; and, even after South Carolina had withdrawn from the Union, she wrote that the American people were "in harmony with the great natural laws."[9]

Miss Sedgwick's intense belief in the democratic ex-periment lay behind her absorption with American ma-terials in her fiction—an aspect of her writings which especially attracted Cooper and Bryant.[10] Among her best-known contemporaries, Irving spent much of the 1820's writing tales and sketches with European settings and characters; and Cooper began his career with *Precaution* (1820) in which he described English society. On the other hand, as Bryant wrote in his review of *Redwood*, this novel was "a conclusive argument, that the writers of fiction of which the scene is laid in familiar and domes-tic life, have a rich and varied field before them in the United States."[11]

Although Miss Sedgwick's regionalism—her concen-tration on New England manners, scenery, and history—must not be forgotten, it is equally important to remember that she was more than just a regionalist; after all, South-erners as well as Yankees are among the central characters in *Redwood*, part of which is set not in New England but rather in Lebanon, one of New York's popular resorts. Furthermore, *The Linwoods* portrays New Yorkers during the Revolution, and both *Clarence* and *Married or Single?* are set in the New York of the mid-nineteenth century. Miss Sedgwick's concern with American ma-terials is, as Tremaine McDowell noted in *The Literary*

History of the United States, one of the more interesting aspects of her novels.[12]

Miss Sedgwick's Americanism led her to write didactic tales in which she attempted to show laborers what manners were necessary if "farmers and mechanics [were] to range with the highest in the land"; for, as a faithful adherent to democracy, she wished to see an era of social equality in America. She believed, in the words of one of the characters in *Home,* that "there is nothing that tends more to the separation into classes than difference of manners."[13] However, while she wished to see social equality between classes, she did not desire equality of the sexes; indeed, her desire to maintain a separation of the sexes is one of the more prominent aspects of her fiction. All her heroines are provided with husbands, and many of these heroines—Jane Elton, Ellen Bruce, Gertrude Clarence, for example—are marked by passive, submissive characters. Yet Miss Sedgwick could attract favorable attention from feminists like Margaret Fuller; for the author of *Hope Leslie* not only showed some independent, self-willed, and courageous women in her fiction but also had succeeded professionally in an age when women were supposed to spend their lives raising children and fulfilling domestic duties.

However, Miss Sedgwick also attributed her professional success to her brothers' encouragement and influence; and, although she concluded *Hope Leslie* with the statement that "marriage is not *essential* to the contentment, the dignity, or the happiness of woman," she wrote shortly afterwards that she "would not advise any one to remain unmarried."[14] Although she wrote *Married or Single?* to demonstrate that marriage was not essential to a woman's happiness, she provided her independent-minded heroine in that novel with a husband. In *Means and Ends,* she advised women to raise children, clean house, and avoid professions such as law, which she felt traditionally belonged to men. Nor did she believe women should vote, and she criticized Margaret Fuller for her "theorizing," "self-esteem," and "egotism"—but then added that "all her conduct after she . . . began the action of life in the accustomed channels was admirable, her Italian life [including her marriage] beautiful."[15] Miss Sedgwick's attitude toward the place of women in society was clearly ambiguous—and helps us understand why she was able to idealize in her fiction women as different as the passive Jane Elton in *A New-England Tale*, the devoted housewife Mrs. Barclay in *Home*, and the entirely independent and self-reliant Hope Leslie.

Miss Sedgwick's ambiguous attitude toward women's rights and her simplistic remedies for curing social inequalities make her appear hopelessly dated as an analyst of social life. On the other hand, any study of early American literature must take into account a number of her decidedly positive achievements. Her delineation of American manners must be noted as well as her value as a regionalist, portraying the history, religion, scenery, manners, and customs of New England long before these subjects provided the substance of works by Harriet Beecher Stowe and Sarah Orne Jewett. Furthermore, it must not be forgotten that her simple and straightforward prose style is eminently more readable than is much of the complex, baroque, often tortured prose found throughout Cooper's writings; and her women are more credible than the more passive and genteel of his females. Because Cooper's imagination provided him with a wider range of subjects for his fiction, modern criticism will continue to find more of interest in his works than Miss Sedgwick's. However, any study of early American literature which makes note of Cooper's achievement must also mention not only Miss Sedgwick's substantial reputation but also her abilities in characterizing women, delineating American manners, and portraying the history, religion, scenery, manners, and customs of her native New England.

Notes and References

Chapter One

1. Oliver Wendell Holmes, *Elsie Venner: A Romance* (New York, 1961), p.16.

2. Henry Ward Beecher, *Star Papers; or, Experiences of Art and Nature* (New York, 1855), p. 181.

3. Nathaniel Hawthorne, *A Wonder Book, The Centenary Edition of the Works of Nathaniel Hawthorne* (Columbus, Ohio; 1972), VII, 169.

4. Evert A. and George L. Duyckinck, *Cyclopedia of American Literature* (New York, 1856), II, 242.

5. Clark W. Bryan, *The Berkshire Book* (Great Barrington, Mass.; 1887), p. 29. Henry Dwight Sedgwick, Jr., "Reminiscences of Literary Berkshire," *The Century Magazine,* L (August, 1895), 565.

6. Margaret Fuller, *Women in the Nineteenth Century* (Boston, 1855), p. 163.

7. Washington Irving, *Margaret Davidson* (Boston, 1857), p. 17.

8. Alexander Cowie, *The Rise of the American Novel* (New York, 1951), p. 202. Michael Davitt Bell, "History and Romance Convention in Catharine Sedgwick's *Hope Leslie,*" *American Quarterly,* XXII (Summer, 1970), 214.

9. Mary E. Dewey, ed., *Life and Letters of Catharine M. Sedgwick* (New York, 1871), pp. 153, 187. The Dewey collection is the source of most of the biographical information in this book. Miss Dewey had access to most of Miss Sedgwick's important letters and journals, and her selections from them are unusually judicious. The manuscript letters which she used are now in the library of the Massachusetts Historical Society, Boston, Massachusetts.

10. *Clarence; or, A Tale of Our Own Times* (Philadelphia, 1830), I, 50.

11. *Life and Letters,* p. 38. Penelope was Miss Sedgwick's father's third wife. All of his children were by his second wife,

Pamela Dwight. His first, Elizabeth Mason, died after a brief marriage.

12. *Ibid.*, p. 80.

13. Sarah Cabot Sedgwick and Christina Sedgwick Marquand, *Stockbridge: 1739–1939: A Chronicle* (Great Barrington, Mass.; 1939), p. 171.

14. *Life and Letters*, p. 26.

15. *A New-England Tale* (New York, 1822), p. 58.

16. *Life and Letters*, pp. 46–47.

17. *Ibid.*, pp. 43–44.

18. *Ibid.*, p. 67.

19. *Ibid.*, p. 56.

20. *Ibid.*, p. 45.

21. *Ibid.*, p. 41.

22. Cowie, *Rise of the American Novel*, p. 210.

23. Richard E. Welch, Jr., *Theodore Sedgwick: Federalist* (Middlebury, Conn.; 1965), p. 7.

24. *Life and Letters*, p. 24.

25. *Ibid.*, p. 30.

26. Welch, *Theodore Sedgwick*, p. 39.

27. *Life and Letters*, p. 35.

28. *Ibid.*, pp. 49–50.

29. Francois de La Rochefoucauld-Liancourt, *Travels through the United States of North America* (London, 1799), p. 418.

30. S. C. Sedgwick, *Stockbridge*, p. 172.

31. *Ibid.*, p. 175.

32. Richard E. Welch, Jr., "Mumbet and Judge Sedgwick: A Footnote to the Early History of Massachusetts Justice," *The Boston Bar Journal*, VII (January, 1964), 14.

33. *Life and Letters*, p. 41.

34. *Ibid.*, p. 42.

35. William Cullen Bryant and Sydney Howard Gray, *A Popular History of the United States* (New York, 1881), IV, 261.

36. *Life and Letters*, p. 61.

37. Elizabeth F. Ellet, *Queens of American Society* (New York, 1867), p. 93.

38. *Life and Letters*, p. 29.

39. *Ibid.*, p. 27.

40. *Ibid.*, p. 35.

41. *Ibid.*, p. 102.

42. *Ibid.*, p. 109.

43. *Ibid.*, p. 160.

44. *Ibid.*, p.112.

45. Fredrika Bremer, *The Homes of the New World: Impressions of America*, trans. Mary Howitt (New York, 1853), II, 596.

46. Perry Miller, *The Raven and the Whale* (New York, 1956), pp. 280–91; Leon Howard, *Herman Melville* (Berkeley and Los Angeles, 1951), pp. 154-60; Randall Stewart, *Nathaniel Hawthorne* (New Haven, Conn.; 1948), p. 107.

47. Jay Leyda, *The Melville Log: A Documentary Life of Herman Melville, 1819–1891* (New York, 1951), I, 385.

48. Frances Anne Kemble, *Records of Later Life* (London, 1882), p. 101; Maunsell B. Field, *Memories of Many Men and of Some Women* (New York, 1875), pp. 201–02; Henry Dwight Sedgwick Jr., "Reminiscences of Literary Berkshire," pp. 552–68.

49. *Life and Letters,* p. 230.

50. *Ibid.,* p. 84.

51. William Cullen Bryant, "Reminiscences of Miss Sedgwick," *Life and Letters,* p. 441.

52. *Ibid.,* p. 261.

Chapter Two

1. Henry Wheeler Shaw [Josh Billings], "Live Yankees," *Josh Billings on Ice, and Other Things* (New York, 1870), p. 21.

2. Quoted in Birdsall, *Berkshire County,* p. 260.

3. Orville Dewey, *Autobiography and Letters,* ed. Mary E. Dewey (Boston, 1884), p. 38.

4. Timothy Dwight, *Travels in New-England and New-York* (London, 1823), II, 361.

5. David Dudley Field, *A History of the County of Berkshire* (Pittsfield, Mass.; 1829), p. 147.

6. Quoted in Anonymous, *The Berkshire Hills* (New York, 1939), p. 116.

7. *Life and Letters,* p. 101.

8. *Ibid.,* p. 60.

9. Stephen West, *Sermons, on the Mosaic Account of Creation: The Serpent's Temptation of Our First Parents, and on Their Exclusion from the Garden of Eden* (Stockbridge, Mass.; 1809), p. 60.

10. Electa F. Jones, *Stockbridge, Past and Present: or, Records of an Old Mission* (Stockbridge, Mass.; 1854), p. 233.

11. *Life and Letters,* p. 20.

12. Dewey, p. 154.

13. *Life and Letters,* p. 68.

14. *Ibid.,* pp. 86–87.

15. *Ibid.,* p. 146.

16. *Ibid.*, pp. 94–95.

17. *Ibid.*, p. 157.

18. *Ibid.*, pp. 150–51.

19. *A New-England Tale* (2nd ed., New York, 1822), p. 14. The second edition differs from the first in that it contains an additional preface and lacks the original subtitle, *Sketches of New-England Characters and Manners*.

20. *Ibid.*, p. 18.

21. *Ibid.*, p. 21.

22. *Ibid.*, p. 39.

23. *Ibid.*, p. 66.

24. *Ibid.*, p. 71.

25. *Ibid.*, p. 80.

26. *Ibid.*, p. 97.

27. *Ibid.*, p. 265.

28. *Ibid.*, p. 132.

29. *Life and Letters*, p. 152.

30. James Fenimore Cooper, review of *A New-England Tale, Early Critical Essays* (1820–22), ed. James F. Beard, Jr. (Gainesville, Fla.; 1955), p. 97. The review originally appeared in *The Literary and Scientific Repository and Critical Review*, IV (May, 1822), 336–70.

31. Jennette Tandy, *Crackerbox Philosophers in American Humor and Satire* (Port Washington, N.Y.; 1964), p. 40.

32. *A New-England Tale*, p. 50.

33. Colonel W. H. Phillips, "Sketch of 'Crazy Sue,'" *The Berkshire Hills*, I (October, 1900), 3.

34. *Ibid.*, p. 3.

35. Further information on "Crazy Sue" can be found in Colonel W. H. Phillips, "More Anecdotes of 'Crazy Sue,'" *The Berkshire Hills*, I (December, 1900), p. 12.

36. Anon. Review, "A New-England Tale," *The Monthly Review*, N.S., CI (May, 1823), 105.

37. *A New-England Tale*, p. vii.

38. *Ibid.*, p. viii.

39. Matthew Buckham, "Lenox as a Jungle for Literary Lions," *Taghconic; or, Letters and Legends about Our Summer Home*, ed. J. E. A. Smith (Boston, 1852), pp. 99–100.

40. *A New-England Tale and Miscellanies* (New York, 1852). This edition contains the preface, pp. 14–16, in which Miss Sedgwick describes her novel in rather unflattering terms and says that its only real importance lies in its historical value.

41. *Life and Letters*, p. 152.

42. *Ibid.*, pp. 152–53.

Chapter Three

1. Anon. Review, *"Redwood,"* *The Atlantic Magazine,* I (July 7, 1924), 236.

2. Charles I. Glicksberg, "Bryant and the Sedgwick Family," *Americana Illustrated,* XXXI (October, 1937), 629.

3. *Redwood, A Tale* (New York, 1824), I, 209.

4. Cowie, p. 202.

5. William Cullen Bryant, review of *Redwood,* *The North American Review,* XI (April, 1825), 268.

6. *Redwood,* I, 258.

7. Harriet Martineau, "Miss Sedgwick's Works," *The London and Westminster Review,* Am. ed., XXVIII (October, 1837), 23.

8. *Redwood,* I, 78.

9. *Ibid.,* I, 79.

10. *Ibid.,* I, 15, 125.

11. *Ibid.,* I, 185.

12. *Ibid.,* I, 120, 123.

13. *Ibid.,* I, 124.

14. *Ibid.,* II, 165.

15. *Ibid.,* I, 115.

16. *Ibid.,* I, 115–16.

17. *Ibid.,* II, 253.

18. *Ibid.,* I, 155.

19. *Ibid.,* II, 5.

20. *Ibid.,* I, 213.

21. *Ibid.,* I, 184.

22. *Ibid.,* I, 266.

23. *Ibid.,* I, 32.

24. *Ibid.,* I, 32–33.

25. *Ibid.,* I, 34.

26. *A New-England Tale,* p. 82.

27. *Redwood,* I, 260.

28. *Ibid.,* I, 31–32.

29. *Ibid.,* I, 31.

30. *Ibid.,* I, 123.

31. *Ibid.,* II, 143; I, 123.

32. *Ibid.,* I, 123.

33. *Ibid.,* II, 41–42.

34. *Ibid.,* II, 37.

35. *Ibid.,* II, 35.

36. *Ibid.,* I, 129.

37. *Ibid.,* II, 37.

38. *Ibid.,* II, 22.

39. *Ibid.,* I, 88; II, 17.

40. *Ibid.*, I, 94.

41. *Ibid.*, I, 96; II, 128.

42. *Ibid.*, II, 21.

43. *Ibid.*, II, 54, 18, 102.

44. *Ibid.*, II, 110.

45. *Ibid.*, I, 212.

46. *Ibid.*, I, 258.

47. *Ibid.*, II, 110.

48. *Ibid.*, I, vii.

49. Caroline S. Kirkland, "Catharine Sedgwick," *Homes of American Authors* (New York, 1854), p. 160.

50. *Life and Letters*, p. 169.

51. Bryant, review of *Redwood*, p. 246.

52. *Ibid.*, p. 248.

53. *Life and Letters*, p. 168.

54. *Ibid.*, p. 169.

55. John S. Hart, *The Female Prose Writers of America* (Philadelphia, 1852), p. 18.

56. Harold E. Mantz, *French Criticism of American Literature before 1850* (New York, 1917), p. 43.

57. *Life and Letters*, p. 172.

58. Anon. Review, *"Hints to My Countrymen," The North American Review*, XIV (October, 1826), 144.

59. Theodore Sedgwick, Jr., *Hints to My Countrymen* (New York, 1826), p. 144.

60. Henry Dwight Sedgwick, "The Common Law," *The North American Review*, I (October, 1824), 416–17.

61. Anon. Review, *"The Deformed Boy," The North American Review*, XIV (July, 1826), 212.

Chapter Four

1. John Higginson, "An Attestation to Mather's Church-History of New England," in Cotton Mather, *Magnalia Christi Americana; or, The Ecclesiastical History of New-England* (Hartford, Conn.; 1855), I, 13.

2. John Greenleaf Whittier, "Biographical Introduction," *The Letters of Lydia Maria Child*, ed. H. W. Sewall (Boston, 1883), pp. vi–vii.

3. H. W. Sewall, *The Letters of Lydia Maria Child* (Boston, 1883), p. 5.

4. Harriet Vaughan Cheney, *A Peep at the Pilgrims in 1636* (Boston, 1824), II, 276.

5. For further information concerning novels set in colonial America, see Ernest E. Leisy, *The American Historical Novel* (Norman, Okla.; 1950), and Adelheid Staehelin-Wackernagel, *The Puritan Settler in the American Novel before the Civil War* (Bern, Switzerland; 1961).

6. *Hope Leslie; or, Early Times in the Massachusetts* (New York, 1842), I, 210. All references are to this edition unless otherwise noted. Mather, I, 25.

7. Mather, I, 118, 552.

8. Benjamin Trumbull, *A Complete History of Connecticut* (New Haven, Conn.; 1818), I, 69.

9. *Ibid.*, I, 76, 80.

10. William Hubbard, *A Narrative of the Indian Wars in New-England* (Brattleborough, Vt.; 1814), p. 46.

11. John Winthrop, *Journal: "A History of New England" (1630–1649)* (New York, 1959), I, 229.

12. Hubbard, p. 47.

13. *Hope Leslie* (1st ed., New York, 1827), I, v. "The antiquarian reader will perceive that some liberties have been taken with the received accounts of Sir Philip (or Sir Christopher) Gardiner; and a slight variation has been allowed in the chronology of the Pequod War."

The first edition of *Hope Leslie* includes a preface not reprinted in the Harper and Brothers edition. Also, the first volume of the first edition—published by White, Gallaher, and White—ends with Chapter XI; the Harper and Brothers edition ends with Chapter XII. The Harper and Brothers edition—which remained in print for more than thirty years — is more frequently encountered in libraries and second-hand book stores than the White, Gallaher, and White edition; therefore, I have chosen to use the Harper edition for reference whenever possible.

14. *Ibid.*, I, 15.

15. Jones, p. 82.

16. *Life and Letters*, p. 19. See also Jones, pp. 82–83.

17. *Life and Letters*, pp. 129–30. Contrary to Miss Sedgwick's account, Eunice did not lose "all recollection of her parents," but such a loss happens to Faith in *Hope Leslie*.

18. Williams, known as Chief Onwarenhiiaki among the Indians, is generally considered to have been the son of Konwatewenteta and Caughnawaga Chief Tehoragwanegen, also known as Thomas Williams. This Williams was the son of Mary (or Sarah) Arosen (or de Rogers)—it all depends on which account is read—wife of a Doctor Williams, an Englishman; and the daughter of Eunice Williams. But to retrace our steps, there are

others who would claim that Chief Onwarenhiiaki was not the son of Konwatewenteta and Caughnawaga Chief Tehoragwanegen but Louis XVII of France, alias the Lost Dauphin. For more relative to this somewhat confused affair, see John H. Hanson, *The Lost Prince* (New York, 1854).

19. John Williams, *The Redeemed Captive Returning to Zion* (Greenfield, Mass.; 1800), p. 9.

20. *Ibid.*, pp. 46–47.

21. Many books and articles concern Eunice Williams and her family, but see especially Alexander Medlicott, Jr., "Return to this Land of Light: A Plea to an Unredeemed Captive," *The New England Quarterly*, XXXVIII (June, 1965), 202-16; Howard H. Peckham, *Captured by Indians; True Tales of Pioneer Survivors* (New Brunswick, N.J.; 1954); Stephen W. Williams, *The Genealogy and History of the Family of Williams* (Greenfield, Mass.; 1847).

22. Medlicott, p. 202.

23. *Hope Leslie*, 1st ed., I, v.

24. Jones, pp. 9–10.

25. *Redwood*, II, 74.

26. *Hope Leslie*, 1st ed., I, v.

27. *Hope Leslie*, I, 15. All future references to the novel are, like this one, to the Harper and Brothers edition.

28. *Ibid.*, I, 4.

29. *Ibid.*, I, 5.

30. *Ibid.*, I, 15.

31. *Ibid.*, I, 19.

32. Hubbard, p. 16.

33. *Hope Leslie*, I, 80.

34. A picture of the attack on Bethel appeared in *The Columbian Magazine*, V (June, 1846), with an accompanying description, pp. 280–81. This illustration is reproduced, facing the title page, in the edition of *Hope Leslie* published by the Garrett Press (New York, 1969). The original picture was by T. H. Matteson, a widely popular artist at the time; and it shows Magawisca valiantly attempting to hold back three savages. Mrs. Fletcher is pictured with seven children in front of her Bethel home. This picture appeared as one in a series of scenes from American literature; other scenes in this series were taken from the works of Irving and Cooper.

35. *Hope Leslie*, I, 94.

36. Elizabeth F. Ellet, *Rambles about the Country* (New York, 1847), pp. 97–98.

37. Cowie, p. 205.

38. *Hope Leslie*, I, 235.

39. *Ibid.*, II, 241.

40. Charles Francis Adams, *Three Episodes of Massachusetts History* (Boston, 1896), I, 250–51.

41. Winthrop, II, 153.

42. *Ibid.*, II, 151.

43. *Hope Leslie*, II, 94.

44. *Ibid.*, I, 144.

45. *Ibid.*, I, 35.

46. *Ibid.*, II, 41; I, 197.

47. *Ibid.*, II, 55.

48. Timothy Flint, review of *Hope Leslie*, *The Western Monthly Review*, I (September, 1827), 295.

49. *Hope Leslie*, II, 2.

50. *Ibid.*, I, 28.

51. *Ibid.*, I, 44.

52. *Ibid.*, II, 232.

53. *Ibid.*, II, 46.

54. *Ibid.*, II, 243.

55. Staehelin-Wackernagel, pp. 82–83.

56. *Hope Leslie*, I, 166.

57. *Ibid.*, I, 167.

58. James Fenimore Cooper, *The Pioneers; or, The Sources of the Susquehanna* (Boston and New York, 1898), p. 303.

59. *Ibid.*, p. 303.

60. *Ibid.*, p. 304.

61. *Ibid.*, p. 476.

62. *Hope Leslie*, II, 263.

63. D. H. Lawrence, *Studies in Classic American Literature* (New York, 1923), pp. 58–59.

64. A discussion of Cooper's contrast between the dark woman (Cora) and the fair heroine (Alice) can be found in Leslie Fiedler's *Love and Death in the American Novel* (Cleveland, 1960), pp. 202-26. Fiedler argues that Cora, unlike her pallid sister, is sexually attractive. If so, this characteristic of the dark woman Miss Sedgwick did not transfer to Hope Leslie. Although Gardiner plans to seduce her, and although the novel does end with her marriage to Everell Fletcher, the men in the novel—excepting Gardiner—are somewhat more interested in her virtuous character than in any other aspect of her nature.

65. Mark Twain, "Fenimore Cooper's Literary Offenses," *North American Review*, CLXI (July, 1895), 11–12.

66. Mark Twain, "Fenimore Cooper's Further Literary Offenses," *New England Quarterly*, XIX (September, 1896), 300.

67. Mark Twain, "Fenimore Cooper's Literary Offenses," p. 3.

68. James Fenimore Cooper, *The Last of the Mohicans* (Boston and New York, 1898), p. 108.

69. *Hope Leslie*, II, 99.

70. Sarah Josepha Hale, *Woman's Record* (New York, 1853), p. 777.

71. Frances Trollope, *Domestic Manners of the Americans* (New York, 1960), pp. 315 and 178.

72. Donald Grant Mitchell, *American Lands and Letters* (New York, 1899), p. 254.

73. Miss Mitford's comment is quoted in R. DeWitt Mallary, *Lenox and the Berkshire Highlands* (New York, 1902), p. 112.

74. Mrs. Lydia Howard (Huntley) Sigourney, *Scenes in My Native Land* (Boston, 1845), pp. 200–01.

75. Anon. Review, *"Hope Leslie," The North American Review*, XXVI (April, 1828), 411.

76. *Ibid.*, pp. 412–13, 420.

77. Anon. Review, *"Merry-Mount," The North American Review*, LXVIII (January, 1849), p. 205.

78. *Life and Letters*, p. 187.

79. *Ibid.*, p. 198.

Chapter Five

1. Trollope, p. 47.

2. Captain Basil Hall, *Travels in North America, in the Years 1827 and 1828* (Edinburgh, 1830), II, 74.

3. *Ibid.*, II, 73.

4. Margaret H. [Mrs. Basil] Hall, *The Aristocratic Journey* (New York, 1931), p. 78.

5. *Ibid.*, p. 78.

6. *Life and Letters*, p. 191.

7. *Letters from Abroad to Kindred at Home* (New York, 1841), I, 14.

8. *Clarence; or, A Tale of Our Own Times* (Philadelphia, 1830), I, 185.

9. *Ibid.*, I, 195.

10. *Ibid.*, I, 227.

11. Anonymous, *The American Code of Manners* (New York, 1880), p. 11. Quoted in Arthur M. Schlesinger, *Learning How to Behave: A Historical Study of American Etiquette Books* (New York, 1946), pp. viii–ix.

12. *Clarence*, I, 239–40.

13. *Life and Letters*, p. 205.

14. *Ibid.*, p. 200–01.

15. Catharine Maria Sedgwick, MS, letter to John Vaughan, dated April 11, 1836, in the Charles Roberts Autograph Collection of the Haverford College Library.

16. Bryan, *The Book of Berkshire*, p. 31.

17. Elizabeth Dwight [Mrs. Charles] Sedgwick, *A Talk with My Pupils* (New York, 1862), pp. 39–40.

18. John Marshall, MS, letter to Polly Marshall, dated February 7, 1831, in the Rucker Collection in the University of Virginia Library.

19. *The Linwoods; or, "Sixty Years Since" in America* (New York, 1861), II, 266.

20. *Ibid.*, I, 118.

21. *Ibid.*, II, 257.

22. *Ibid.*, II, 257.

23. *Ibid.*, I, 198.

24. *Ibid.*, I, 78, 71.

25. *Ibid.*, II, 284.

26. *Ibid.*, I, 259.

27. *Life and Letters*, p. 249.

28. Catharine Maria Sedgwick, MS, letter to Charles Sedgwick, dated January 15, 1822, in the Catharine Maria Sedgwick Papers of the Massachusetts Historical Society.

29. *The Linwoods*, I, 89-90. This characterization occurs in the episode in which Eliot Lee leaves his family to fight in the Revolution.

30. Compare the description of the Reverend Wilson with the following description of the Reverend Stephen West. The passage is taken from Miss Sedgwick's autobiography—first published in the *Life and Letters*, p. 61—and is dated 1853. This date suggests that the description of the Reverend West was not written until nearly twenty years after *The Linwoods* was published, but it is so similar to the description of the Reverend Wilson in that novel that possibly either the comments on the Reverend West were written long before the date on the manuscript of the autobiography suggests, or they were written shortly after Miss Sedgwick had reread her characterization of the Reverend Wilson.

I will try to sketch the doctor's outward man for you. He was not, I think, above five feet in height. His person was remarkably well-made and erect, and I think the good little polemic was slightly vain of it, for I remember his garments fitted accurately, and nice hose (in summer always of black silk) displayed a handsome calf and ankle, and his

shining black shoes and silver buckles impressed even my careless
eye. . . . His knock at the "east door" was as recognizable as his
voice; that opened to him, he came in, and taking off his hat, saluted each
member of the family, down to the youngest, with the exact ceremony,
and something of the grace of a French courtier; he then walked up to
the table between the two front windows, deposited the three-cornered
beaver, put his gloves in his hat, and his silver-headed cane in the corner,
and then, taking a little comb from his pocket, he smoothed down his
thin locks, so that every numbered hair on his head lay in its appointed
place.

31. Anon. Review, "The Linwoods," The Athenaeum, no. 411
(Setpember 12, 1835), pp. 693–94. Harriet Martineau, "Miss
Sedgwick's Works," The London and Westminster Review,
American ed., XXVIII (October, 1837), p. 30.

32. Anon. Review, "The Linwoods," The North American Review, XLII (January, 1836), p. 160. Mitchell, p. 254.

33. Ibid., p. 194. A bluestocking—or member of "a Blue Congress" is a woman who is pedantic in her literary and intellectual tastes.

Chapter Six

1. Clarence, II, 98.

2. Catharine Maria Sedgwick, MS, letter to Horace Mann,
dated January 31 (1846?), in the Catharine Maria Sedgwick
Papers of the Massachusetts Historical Society.

3. Nathaniel Parker Willis, Prose Works (Philadelphia, 1855),
p. 682.

4. John Stafford, The Literary Criticism of "Young America"
(New York, 1967), p. 82.

5. Anon. Review, "Miss Sedgwick" The Poor Rich Man and
the Rich Poor Man, American Quarterly Review, XXI (March, 1837),
18, 20, and 28.

6. Life and Letters, p. 239.

7. Live and Let Live; or, Domestic Service Illustrated (New
York, 1839), dedication page and p. v.

8. Life and Letters, p. 270.

9. Ibid., p. 259.

10. Ibid., p. 260.

11. Ibid., p. 445.

12. Orestes Brownson, review of Means and Ends, The Boston
Quarterly Review, II (July, 1839), 389.

13. Life and Letters, p. 53.

14. Harriet Martineau, Autobiography (London, 1877), II, 67.

15. *Ibid.*, II, 67.

16. *Live and Let Live*, p. 54.

17. *Ibid.*, p. 54.

18. *Home*, new edition (Boston and Cambridge, 1852), p. 1. William Cullen Bryant, *Poetical Works*, ed. Parke Godwin (New York, 1883), I, 31–33.

19. *Home*, p. 4.

20. *Ibid.*, p. 5.

21. *Ibid.*, pp. 13–14.

22. *Ibid.*, p. 3.

23. *Ibid.*, p. 36.

24. *Ibid.*, p. 38.

25. *Ibid.*, p. 40.

26. *Ibid.*, p. 109.

27. *Ibid.*, p. 28.

28. *Ibid.*, p. 39.

29. *Ibid.*, p. 40.

30. *Ibid.*, p. 76.

31. *Ibid.*, p. 115

32. *Ibid.*, p. 120.

33. *Ibid.*, p. 120.

34. Theodore Sedgwick, Jr., *Hints to My Countrymen* (New York, 1826), pp. 129–30.

35. *The Boy of Mount Rhigi* (Boston, 1848), p. 5.

36. *Life and Letters*, p. 310.

37. George William Curtis, "Editor's Easy Chair," *Harper's New Monthly Magazine*, XXXV (October, 1867), p. 665.

38. Richard D. Birdsall, *Berkshire County: A Cultural History* (New Haven, 1959), p. 373.

39. Herman Melville, "Poor Man's Pudding and Rich Man's Crumbs," *Selected Writings of Herman Melville* (New York, 1952), p. 177.

40. Catharine Maria Sedgwick, *Means and Ends; or, Self-Training* (Boston, 1839), p. 13.

41. *Charlie Hathaway; or, The City Clerk and His Sister; and Other Stories* (New York, 1869), p. 21.

42. *Life and Letters*, p. 68.

43. *Ibid.*, p. 299.

44. Lucretia Maria Davidson, *Poetical Remains*, new and revised edition (Boston, 1857), p. 203.

45. *Letters from Abroad to Kindred at Home* (New York, 1841), I, 62.

46. *Ibid.*, I, 61.

47. *Ibid.*, I, 68.

48. Anon. Review, *"Married or Single?" The Athenaeum,* no. 1556 (August 22, 1857), 1057.

49. Henry Fothergill Chorley, *Autobiography, Memoir, and Letters,* compiled by Henry G. Hewlett (London, 1873), I, 280–81.

50. Anon. Review, *"Letters from Abroad to Kindred at Home," The Christian Review,* VI (December, 1841), 632.

51. Fuller, p. 163.

52. *Married or Single?* (New York, 1857), I, vi.

53. *Ibid.,* I, vi.

54. Miss Sedgwick wrote in her preface to *Married or Single?* (I, v) that she had "the fears and faltering of a stranger in appearing before the present public. The generation known to her, and which extended a welcome and a degree of favor to her, has, for the most part, passed away. Most of those friends are gone, whose hearts vibrated (without the vanities or selfishness of personality) to her success, and she is left to feel the chill and dreariness of the "banquet-hall deserted.'"

55. Sister Mary Michael Welsh, *Catharine Maria Sedgwick; Her Position in the Literature and Thought of Her Time up to 1860.* (Washington, 1937), p. 33.

56. *Married or Single?,* I, 206–07.

57. *Memoir of Joseph Curtis, a Model Man* (New York, 1858), p. 192.

58. In his "Reminiscences of Miss Sedgwick"—*Life and Letters,* p. 444—Bryant wrote that *The Linwoods* was Miss Sedgwick's last novel; then, in a footnote, he added that "this is a mistake, but, as it has been put in type, I prefer to correct it in a note." He went on to state that *Married or Single?* was published twenty–two years after *The Linwoods.* He indicated that he knew of some people who liked the later novel, but not that he had read it.

59. Another twenty thousand copies were sold in the five weeks which followed. For a discussion of this novel and its popularity see my Foreword to Maria Cummins, *The Lamplighter* (New York, 1969), pp. iii–v.

60. *Life and Letters,* p. 278.

61. *Ibid.,* p. 367.

62. *Ibid.,* p. 411.

63. Sarah Orne Jewett, *Letters,* ed. Annie Fields (Boston, 1911), pp. 218–19.

64. Curtis, p. 665.

Chapter Seven

1. Anon. Review, "Clarence," *The Literary World*, no. 140 (October 6, 1849), 297. The italics are my own.

3. Hawthorne, p. 196.

3. Anonymous, "A New England Village," *Harper's New Monthly Magazine*, XLIII (November, 1871), 826. Edgar Allan Poe, *The Literati of New York City* (Boston, 1902), p. 108. Curtis, p. 665.

4. Bryant, "Reminiscences of Miss Sedgwick," p. 443.

5. Anonymous, "Literature of the Nineteenth Century: America," *The Athenaeum*, no. 375 (January 1, 1835), 11.

6. *Ibid.*, 11.

7. *Life and Letters*, p. 285.

8. *Ibid.*, pp. 285–86.

9. *Ibid.*, pp. 355 and 389.

10. Cooper, review of *A New-England Tale*, p. 97. Bryant, review of *Redwood*, p. 248.

11. *Ibid.*, p. 248.

12. Tremaine McDowell, "In New England," *Literary History of the United States*, ed. Robert E. Spiller *et al.* (New York, 1953), p. 290.

13. *Home*, pp. 39 and 40.

14. *Hope Leslie*, II, 292. *Life and Letters*, p. 198. For an excellent discussion of the extraordinary emphasis which the nineteenth century gave to marriage, see Barbara Welter, "The Cult of True Womanhood, 1820–1860," *American Quarterly*, XVIII (1966), 151–74.

15. *Life and Letters*, p. 341.

Selected Bibliography

PRIMARY SOURCES

I have marked works of interest with (*), important works (**), and major works (***).

**A New-England Tale*. New York: E. Bliss & E. White, 1822. (novel)
**Redwood*. New York: E. Bliss & E. White, 1824. (novel)
The Travellers. New York: E. Bliss & E. White, 1825. (children's book)
The Deformed Boy. Brookfield, Mass.: E. & G. Merriam, printers; 1826. (children's book)
****Hope Leslie*. New York: White, Gallaher, and White, 1827. (novel)
**Clarence*. Philadelphia: Carey, 1830. (novel)
**The Linwoods*. New York: Harper & Brothers, 1835. (novel)
* *Tales and Sketches*. Philadelphia: Carey, Lea, and Blanchard, 1835. (collection)
** *Home*. Boston: J. Munroe, 1835. (didactic tale)
* *The Poor Rich Man and the Rich Poor Man*. New York: Harper & Brothers, 1836. (didactic tale)
* *Live and Let Live*. New York: Harper & Brothers, 1837. (didactic tale)
A Love-token for Children. New York: Harper & Brothers, 1838. (children's book)
Means and Ends. Boston: Marsh, Capen, Lyon, & Webb, 1839. (children's book)
Lucretia Maria Davidson, in *The Library of American Biography*, ed. Jared Sparks. New York: Harper & Brothers. 1839. (biography)
Letters from Abroad to Kindred at Home. New York: Harper & Brothers, 1841. (travel book)
Tales and Sketches. Second Series. New York: Harper & Brothers, 1844. (collection)

The Morals of Manners. New York: G. P. Putnam, 1846. (children's book)

Facts and Fancies for School-day Reading. New York and London: Wiley & Putnam, 1848. (children's book)

* *The Boy of Mount Rhigi.* Boston: C. H. Peirce, 1848. (children's book)

* *Married or Single?* New York: Harper & Brothers, 1857. (novel)

Memoir of Joseph Curtis. New York: Harper & Brothers, 1858. (biography)

** *Life and Letters,* ed. Mary E. Dewey. New York: Harper & Brothers, 1871. Includes the unfinished autobiography on pp. 13–78.

There have been numerous reprintings of Miss Sedgwick's works. Selections from the various collections of shorter pieces were made and published as new works, although the contents of these books had been previously published in book form. In 1849, G. P. Putnam began publishing a uniform edition of Miss Sedgwick's works, but only three volumes in this series were issued: *Clarence* (1849), *Redwood* (1849), and *A New-England Tale* (1852). These volumes were reissued in 1854 by J. C. Derby (Boston) and Phillips, Sampson, and Company (New York). Harper and Brothers became Miss Sedgwick's publishers in the 1830's and continued to reissue her works. Several of her earliest volumes, including *Hope Leslie* and *The Linwoods,* were still in print as late as the 1870's. *Hope Leslie* and *Redwood* were reprinted by the Garrett Press (New York) in 1969.

The only large collection of Miss Sedgwick's letters is at the Massachusetts Historical Society in Boston. The collection includes the letters which Mary Dewey used in the *Life and Letters.*

Secondary Sources

Bibliographical

GIDEZ, RICHARD BANUS. "A Study of the Works of Catharine Maria Sedgwick." Unpublished dissertation, Ohio State University, 1958. Includes a comprehensive bibliography of Miss Sedgwick's short pieces for magazines and annuals.

WELSH, SISTER MARY MICHAEL. *Catharine Maria Sedgwick: Her Position in the Literature and Thought of Her Time up to 1860.* Washington: The Catholic University of America, 1937. Includes a bibliography of foreign translations of

Miss Sedgwick's works and a bibliography of Miss Sedgwick's contributions to magazines and annuals.

Critical and Biographical Studies

ANONYMOUS. "Literature of the Nineteenth Century: America," *The Athenaeum*, No. 375 (January 3, 1835), 9–11. See entry below.

ANONYMOUS. Review of *Clarence*, *The Literary World*, No. 140 (October 6, 1849), 297–98. *The Athenaeum* and *Literary World* articles are good examples of the highly favorable criticism Miss Sedgwick received during her lifetime from British and American periodicals, respectively.

BEACH, SETH CURTIS. "Catharine Sedgwick," *Daughters of the Puritans*. Boston: American Unitarian Association, 1905. Useful as a *concise* account of the author's life.

BELL, MICHAEL DAVITT. "History and Romance Convention in Catharine Sedgwick's *Hope Leslie*," *American Quarterly*, XXII (Summer, 1970), 213–21. Primarily interesting for its examination of Hope Leslie as Miss Sedgwick's symbol for American liberty and freedom.

BIRDSALL, RICHARD D. "William Cullen Bryant and Catharine Sedgwick—Their Debt to Berkshire," *The New England Quarterly*, XXVIII (September, 1955), 349–71. Interesting study of the New England background of Miss Sedgwick's works.

BIRDSALL, RICHARD D. *Berkshire County: A Cultural History*. New Haven: Yale University Press, 1959. The best book about the Berkshires and about the cultural life of the area in Miss Sedgwick's lifetime. See especially chapters Three ("Heads Full of Divinity"), Four ("A Great Deal of Dissent"), Seven ("The Right to Scribble"), Nine ("New England Character"), and Ten ("The American Lake District").

BROOKS, GLADYS. *Three Wise Virgins*. New York: E. P. Dutton and Co., Inc., 1957. Provides little information not in the *Life and Letters* and *Letters from Abroad to Kindred at Home*.

BROWN, CHARLES H. *William Cullen Bryant*. New York: Charles Scribner's Sons, 1971. Contains much material on Bryant's friendship with Catharine Sedgwick and members of her family.

BRYANT, WILLIAM CULLEN. Review of *Redwood*, *The North American Review*, XI (April, 1825), 245–72. This exceptionally important article emphasizes Miss Sedgwick's use of native American materials. It has been anthologized several times and was reprinted in his *Prose Writings*, ed. Parke Godwin (New York: A. Appleton and Company, 1884).

COWIE, ALEXANDER. *The Rise of the American Novel*. New York: American Book Co., 1951. Best short criticism of Miss Sedgwick's novels.

CUTLER, JAMES TUCKER. "The Literary Associations of Berkshire," *The New England Magazine*, N.S. IX (September, 1893), 3–22. Anecdotes of life in "The American Lake District."

FOSTER, EDWARD HALSEY. "Foreword." *Hope Leslie*. New York: Garrett Press, Inc., 1969. Examines the book not only as a historical novel but also as a novel of manners.

FOSTER, EDWARD HALSEY. "Foreword." *Redwood*. New York: Garrett Press, Inc., 1969. Examines *Redwood* as a novel of manners with a national as well as regional focus.

GIDEZ, RICHARD BANUS. "A Study of the Works of Catharine Maria Sedgwick." Unpublished dissertation, Ohio State University, 1958. Especially important as a study of Miss Sedgwick's works in the traditions of nineteenth-century sentimental literature.

GLICKSBERG, CHARLES I. "Bryant and the Sedgwick Family," *Americana Illustrated*, XXXI (October, 1937), 626–38. Concise examination of Bryant's friendship with Miss Sedgwick and her family.

MALLARY, R. DEWITT. *Lenox and the Berkshire Highlands*. New York: G. P. Putnam's Sons, 1902. Chapter Three ("Catharine Maria Sedgwick: Her Message and Her Work") is a brief survey of Miss Sedgwick's writings by a local historian.

POE, EDGAR ALLAN. Review of *The Linwoods, Literary Criticism*, Vol. I, ed. James A. Harrison. New York: AMS Press, Inc., 1965. Generally more sympathetic account of Miss Sedgwick than that in Poe's *Literati*.

SEDGWICK, HENRY DWIGHT, JR. "Reminiscences of Literary Berkshire," *The Century Magazine*, L (August, 1895), 552–68. Anecdotal history of American Lake District by one of Miss Sedgwick's nephews.

SEDGWICK, SARAH CABOT, and CHRISTINA SEDGWICK MARQUAND. *Stockbridge: 1739–1939: A Chronicle*. Great Barrington, Mass.: The Berkshire Courier, 1939. Superficial survey; does cover aspects of Sedgwick biography and historical background not found elsewhere. See especially Chapter Ten ("The Village Becomes Literary").

STAEHELIN-WACKERNAGEL, ADELHEID. *The Puritan Settler in the American Novel before the Civil War.* Bern, Switzerland: Francke Verlag, 1961. Favorably compares *Hope Leslie* with other nineteenth-century American novels of Puritan life.

STEARNS, BERTHA-MONICA. "Miss Sedgwick Observes Harriet Martineau," *The New England Quarterly*, VII (September, 1934), 533–41. Account of the friendship and disagreements between Miss Sedgwick and Miss Martineau.

WELCH, RICHARD E., JR. *Theodore Sedgwick, Federalist.* Middletown, Conn.: Wesleyan University Press, 1965. Essential for understanding Theodore Sedgwick's political ideals and their effect on his daughter.

WELSH, SISTER MARY MICHAEL. *Catharine Maria Sedgwick: Her Position in the Literature and Thought of Her Time up to 1860.* Washington: The Catholic University of America, 1937. A general study; includes comments on even the least important works. Summarizes the major works, and compares Miss Sedgwick's writings with writings by her contemporaries.

WOODS, DAVID H. *Lenox: Massachusetts Shire Town.* Published by the town of Lenox, Mass., 1969. Pp. 81–87 contain an account of Miss Sedgwick's life in Lenox and a brief analysis of *Redwood.* Treats the novel favorably but is critical of its melodramatic passages.

Index

Index